Prayers on the Wind

Books authored or coauthored by Blaine M. Yorgason and/or Brenton G. Yorgason

Prayers on the Wind
Spiritual Survival in the Last Days
Here Stands a Man
The Warm Spirit
Into the Rainbow
Roger and Sybil Ferguson Biography (private printing)
Sacred Intimacy
Little-Known Evidences of the Book of Mormon
Decision Point
Pardners: Three Stories on Friendship
In Search of Steenie Bergman (Soderberg Series #5)
KING — The Life of Jerome Palmer King (private printing)
The Greatest Quest
Seven Days for Ruby (Soderberg Series #4)
Dirty Socks and Shining Armour — A Tale from Camelot
The Eleven-Dollar Surgery
Becoming
Bfpstk and the Smile Song (out of print)
The Shadow Taker
Tales from the Book of Mormon
Brother Brigham's Gold (Soderberg Series #3)
Ride the Laughing Wind
The Miracle
The Thanksgiving Promise
Chester, I Love You (Soderberg Series #2)
Double Exposure
Seeker of the Gentle Heart
The Krystal Promise
A Town Called Charity, and Other Stories about Decisions
The Bishop's Horse Race (Soderberg Series #1)
And Should We Die
Windwalker (movie version — out of print)
The Windwalker
Others
Charlie's Monument
From First Date to Chosen Mate
Tall Timber (out of print)
Miracles and the Latter-day Teenager (out of print)
From Two to One
From This Day Forth
Creating a Celestial Marriage (textbook)
Marriage and Family Stewardships (textbook)

"Gospel Power Series" by Blaine and Brenton Yorgason

Binding the Lord
The Sword of Testimony
Receiving Answers to Prayer
How to Repent
Satan and His Host
Obtaining Priesthood Power
The Problem with Immorality
Agency, Spiritual Progression, and the Mighty Change
Seeking Wealth
A Gift of Dog Food
To Mothers, from the Book of Mormon
Cory and the Horned Toad

A Novel by
Blaine & Brenton Yorgason

BOOKCRAFT
Salt Lake City, Utah

Library of Congress Catalog Card Number: 91-71322

ISBN 0-88494-790-4

2nd Printing, 1991

Printed in the United States of America

A special thanks to our good friend Mark Eubank for his assistance in making accurate the weather data in this book

Contents

Introduction

As Alma taught the lowly Zoramites, men and women — if they are compelled to be humble — sometimes seek more diligently after the Lord than might otherwise be the case. Many things that are generally stressful in nature compel mortals toward humility. When under stress, men and women who are inclined toward righteousness will grope their way toward a closer relationship with God. Thus, as a means of bringing about this closer relationship, Heavenly Father allows stress-filled experiences to come into our lives.

One such producer of stress in our world is the weather.

Little affects us mortals, wherever we may live upon the earth, as completely as does the weather. Weather conditions are fundamental influences in the production of our foods; in scheduling our recreation; in what we wear; in the planning of work; in types of housing; in the progress or slowdown of business, industry, and transportation; in our successes and our failures; and frequently in the state of our health — physical, mental, emotional, and spiritual. In fact, the psychological effects of weather on the human temperament can be little short of astounding.

The weather's behavior affects the behavior of everything, animate or inanimate, on the earth. It supports life and causes death. It brings joy and grief alike. In all ages of the earth, God has used the weather to bring about his holy purposes—for individuals as well as for entire nations. Such events as the flood of Noah, the great biblical famines, and the storm that altered the very face of the American continents at the crucifixion of Christ were manifestations of the weather.

The climatic zones—such as polar, torrid, and temperate—that encircle the earth are the exclusive works of weather in orderly, departmentalized control of our vast sphere, with the angle of the sun and the air currents masterminding the total pattern.

Generally speaking, all weather begins and is contained in the troposphere, the encircling ocean of air which uses the earth as its floor. The face of the earth becomes disturbed or calm, warm or cool, wet or dry because of the behavior of weather systems within the troposphere. Prevailing wind currents that flow through the troposphere steer the highs and lows, the weather makers that change our weather from clear to stormy and back again. Also, water is drawn from the earth's surface, only to be recycled into clouds and precipitation so that it can once again return to the ground. This cycle is continuous and provides a vital redistribution of the earth's water so that all parts of the world can receive their nourishment. Without water, there would be no weather as we know it.

So what, exactly, is weather? It is the specific condition of temperature, humidity, wind, atmospheric pressure, and precipitation at a given place and time. And because the earth is never still, weather is in a constant state of change.

Although these changes appear to be random, weather is created in an atmosphere that follows exact laws of physics as ordained by God; man simply has not yet found the way to decipher all of God's equations. However, despite the number, diversity, and immensity of the phenomena that go into the making of weather at any moment and place, meteorologists have come to understand weather processes surprisingly well.

Considering these facts, we thought it might be worthwhile to examine one specific—and fairly early—winter cyclonic storm, following its path from its origination in the Gulf of Alaska on Thursday, October 27, 1910, through to its dissipation over the Great Plains some twelve days later. And though the behavior of the storm itself was interesting, what fascinated us were the effects that particular storm might have had upon ten separate Latter-day Saints, individuals of various ages and circumstances who, with their families, happened to be in the path that the storm took.

Thursday, October 27, 1910

The Gulf of Alaska

The early winter storm we will be following has its birth above the vast, cool, watery sweep of ocean known as the Gulf of Alaska. A massive high-pressure system has been in the area, an immense mountain of air that is weighed down heavily with moisture and which has given birth to winds spiraling clockwise around its center. This high-pressure system has been held in position by the far northward sweep of the polar jet stream.

But then, on Thursday, October 27, the jet stream suddenly drops southward, slamming cold arctic air into the nearly static high-pressure area. The clashing air masses create a fast-moving low-pressure system, or cold front, with winds twisting counterclockwise as the front develops into a major storm.

To explain what is happening in layman's terms, a very cold air mass, plowing into a warmer one, behaves much like a gigantic bulldozer. The warm air is driven upward by the colder air as if thrown over the bulldozer's blade top, and deep cumulonimbus clouds may develop along the front of this movement much like dust clouds form where the bulldozer blade breaks the earth. From these clouds, massive amounts of precipitation may fall. This moisture, combined with the high, gusty winds created by rapid temperature changes along the front, as well as by the rota-

tion of the earth, becomes a cyclonic storm such as the one that begins Thursday, October 27, 1910.

All this becomes terribly significant for the young skipper of a fishing trawler, who with his crew is plying the teeming waters of the Gulf of Alaska.

THE FEELING

The *Ginnie Marie* was four hours off the southernmost point of Kachamak Bay, steadily trawling the past summer's fishing grounds on the fourth of a six-day voyage, when the skipper, Steve Argyle, first noticed the gulls. They were noisy as gulls will be, and a small flock still followed the boat's wake. But what he noticed wasn't that. It was the few who were far off, high and seemingly uninterested in the offal from the boat—only now those few gulls weren't so high, nor so far off, and *that* he noticed.

Reaching out, he pulled again on the closest of his two starboard lines, feeling with satisfaction its weight. This would be a good catch, as the last line had been. And this late in the season, too. Coho salmon in October were unusual, but nevertheless here they were, and he was grateful for them.

Glancing toward the sun, he squinted in thought. By rights he ought to have enough day left for three more good casts with each line, perhaps four. And then maybe more after sunset.

But those gulls—

Anxious, he looked once more at the sky and was surprised to see rapidly developing cirrus and cirrocumulus clouds: a moment before there had been nothing but blue sky. Of course, the clouds were just forming, but they were doing so with unusual speed.

The sun hung low in the southwest, and he knew that it would be setting by midafternoon. Even then the darkness that followed was never a true darkness, and in the midst of such a school of fish as they now found themselves, his crew might work for hours and not be hampered by night. Nor would the journey back to port be dangerous. Always it seemed that they sailed out in the dark, and always they managed to return.

Of course in the bright, brief summer, things were opposite, and Steve Argyle smiled as he thought of it. Daylight for almost twenty-four hours, or darkness for that long. What a land of contrasts!

Even after a dozen years he was not used to it, but this was the way of things for those who fished the teeming waters of the Gulf of Alaska, and he was willing to accept it.

Glancing aft, Steve watched where the salmon were thrashing water. *Klop.* A flash of silver. Bubbles. A series of concentric rings that ran away in ripples until they merged into other widening rings. They were everywhere, until the sea seemed full of them, alive with them.

As he well knew, the salmon was a surface fish, its average swimming depth being seldom below four fathoms. It broke water when it fed, when it played, when it ran in schools. Thus, it was not difficult to determine where they were, and where it would be best to set his lines and make a run for them.

But the clouds, and those low-flying gulls—

Leaning over the gunwale where the long pole rested, he tugged at the outer line, pondering. He was definitely uneasy, almost jumpy, and that was not like him. Nor was it like him to be distracted when there was work to be done, casting his eyes skyward after a bunch of gulls when he had no real reason to do so. Yet whether it was like himself or not, he had done so, and was just as surely feeling a nervous, hollow feeling, as if something was going wrong that he had no power to control.

Steve Argyle had experienced that feeling once before, he remembered, during a dismal day in his youth that had ended only when word had reached him of his mother's accidental death. Could that be it, he wondered? Could there be a problem with his sweetheart, Ginnie Marie, or with one of their five children?

Briefly he bowed his head in prayer, pleading for his family's protection while he was at sea. And though he felt a little better when he again opened his eyes, the sense of emptiness almost instantly returned. He just could not put his finger on the reason for it.

"Skipper?"

Turning, Steve glanced quizzically at the young man who had spoken—a tall, thin, humorous individual named Ron Simington. Ron was manning the wheel up in the wheelhouse, but at the moment he stood stooped in the open doorway.

"Aye, lad?"

"Mackerel sky forming, Skipper. And the swells are growing. Before long we'll have wind."

Nodding briefly, the skipper turned again to the line and began reeling it in, his body moving easily with the pitching boat. Wind, was it? Interesting that the lad had noticed the sky as well. Might that be what he was feeling?

Moments later, breathing heavily but still engrossed in trying to understand what was troubling him, Steve Argyle stood to as his other hand gaffed another salmon aboard.

"Zeke?" Steve asked softly then, as he watched the swirling clouds and the distant gulls.

Standing upright, Ezekial Kimball, an old salt who had fished the gulf for forty years, looked quickly at him and then away, back down at the line.

Steve glanced then at Zeke, and once again felt an awe of the old man that he doubted he would ever get over. There the old salt stood, bareheaded, his sleeves rolled up above his elbows, standing in hip boots of rubber on a deck wet and slippery with water and fish slime, amid piles of gleaming salmon, and he was whistling the same nameless tune he had been whistling for the past eleven hours, and working just as hard.

Despite his age, Zeke rose wearily from his bunk every morning at three so that he and the rest of the crew could be on the grounds during that gray hour between dawn and sunrise when schooling salmon best strike the trawling spoon. In all, he spent the bulk of eighteen hours a day hauling five one-hundred-and-fifty-foot lines, each weighted with from six to fifteen pounds of lead. He also took care of the gear and picarooned most of the fish into the hold. And still he whistled. The man seemed indefatigable, and the skipper wondered at that. He truly did.

"Are the gulls lower, Zeke?" Steve finally asked. "Have you noticed?"

"That they be," Ezekial Kimball growled as he turned and scuttled toward the stern. "They be lower, and I've noticed. So too have I noticed the swell."

"Storm, is it?"

"With a growing swell, mackerel sky, and the gulls lower? Aye, Skipper. We be in for a bit of a blow, we be."

"Is there time for another cast, do you think?"

Ezekial Kimball looked at the skipper, considering the question. Steve Argyle was young in the fisheries, as far as skippers went, and that was against him. He was also a land-lubber, hailing from down below in the States, and had not grown up at the helm of a boat. In fact other fishermen had warned old Zeke against shipping with him. But he was quick, this one, and not so filled with pride that he couldn't ask for help, or for advice. Besides that, the *Ginnie Marie* was a fine new trawler, a tight craft with a reliable gas engine, and she was a joy to be aboard. Those two things had helped old Zeke to make his decision.

There had also been a third reason, but old Zeke was still at a loss to explain it. Nonetheless, it was there. There was that about the skipper, some undefinable sense that Zeke had never been able to quite put his finger on, that made a man feel confident, safe, secure. What it was, Zeke did not know. He only knew it was real, and he felt it. And that indescrib-able *something* had tipped the balance in favor of his ship-ping with young Steve Argyle.

And it had turned out that the skipper, inexperienced though he might be, had a real nose for fish. Only two other boats were on the fishing grounds these days, and they had both followed Argyle out, having learned the same valuable lesson that Zeke had learned—Steve Argyle could find fish. No one else even suspected that coho salmon were to be had this late in the season. But the skipper had had himself a hunch, they had sailed, and for four straight days now they had done well, trawling back and forth across the grounds, with amazing catches every run.

Each night in the cove where they weighed anchor they had picarooned their catch aboard the Fox Bay Cannery's carrier, and each night the cannery representative had paid the skipper better money for the *Ginnie Marie*'s fish, exclaim-ing as he did so that he had not seen such fine coho all season long. Nor, for that matter, had Ezekial Kimball.

For a moment Zeke stood, his hand rubbing an old gaff wound on his thigh, thinking. In the spring—when life took on a new prompting—the chinook, or king, and the blueback salmon first showed in the gulf. Neither the blueback nor the chinook could be taken by net or bait, unless the bait was a small live herring. They could only be taken in commercial quantities by a spinner or a wobbling spoon hook of silver, copper, or brass drawn through the water at a slow speed.

In the summer the chinook and blueback runs tapered off, but the first few days of September ushered in the annual coho and humpback runs on their way to their spawning grounds. They did not school along island shores, feeding upon tiny herring. Instead they grouped in squadrons and swept through the gulf on their way to their spawning streams. Oh, they might loaf briefly in the mouths of the rivers, but soon they would be gone again, swiftly moving up-stream, giving fishermen little chance to make a profit from their catch.

By October they were gone, and all that were left were the dog salmon, great-toothed slimy fish that were canned for ex-port—for cheap trade. These still brought profit for the fisher-men at the canneries, but it was a smaller profit, and many fishermen simply did not bother going out.

But not the *Ginnie Marie*, Ezekial Kimball thought wryly as he continued to rub his leg. The skipper had felt there would be fish, good fish, and now here they were in a run of coho the likes of which he had never seen, at least not this late in the season.

But as for the weather?

Ezekial Kimball looked skyward, watching through squinted eyes the scuttling clouds and the gulls, dark against the lighter background. The clouds were moving fast, grow-ing fast. So too were the swells. And the gulls, all of them, were definitely flying lower over the water. But still—

At that moment the *Ginnie Marie* was struck by a gust of air, terribly cold air, that sent a shiver through the old man. Froth from the white-capped wave tops flew at him, and he saw that the skipper had paused once again in his work to look skyward.

"Skipper," old Zeke growled as he grabbed a gaff and swung down beside him, "I've a feeling in me, a bad feeling. This one's coming hard. Those clouds be coming in from the north and west, and before this day be out, we'll be in for a real blow. First big storm of the winter, I be thinking. Was it me, I'd crank up the engine and run for it."

Tersely the skipper nodded. "And you?" he asked, look-ing upward at the unusually solemn Ron Simington. "What would you do, lad? Should we run for it or stay?"

"I'm with Zeke, sir," the young man replied. "My father always said that the fish could wait, but there were days when a fisherman shouldn't. A mackerel sky means wind, Skipper. A real blow. And now we have the mare's tails to boot. There'll be a storm coming, sir. To tell you the truth, this feels like one of those days when the fishermen shouldn't wait."

"And the gear?"

"Lines are expensive," Ron Simington replied slowly, "as are lures and hooks. And all of ours are heavy with fish. I think that there will be time to bring them in and empty them."

"And you, Zeke?" Steve Argyle asked quietly.

"Bring them in?" the old man replied as he again squinted skyward. "Aye. We could. And like the lad says, the gear be expensive. I think we can do it, Skipper. Ye've a tight craft here, and a fine engine. If it comes to it, we can run before a blow. Aye, my vote is to save the gear and the catch."

Anxiously Steve Argyle looked across the sea, trying to determine what the men on the other two distant ships might be thinking. But so far as he could tell, they seemed to be holding steady. Even through the glass he could detect no unusual activity upon deck.

That was how he wanted it on his own ship, too—steady as she goes. He was certain a storm was building, but confound it, those lines and other gear were terribly costly, and he could ill afford to lose all of them. Nor could he afford to lose the fine catch he was certain was on the lines. Within an hour they could have them all in and be on their way—and for the life of him he couldn't see how an hour would make that much difference.

Yet deep within his stomach the feeling of anxiety was growing stronger, and it was as though some nameless dread was threatening to overpower him altogether.

"What's the word, Skipper?" old Zeke asked with a wry grin. "Do we fish or cut bait?"

"You mean 'cut lines'?" Steve Argyle responded with a return smile, thin but sincere. "Zeke, I honestly don't know how to answer you. Start reeling in the stern line, and give me another minute or two to think this through.

"Lad," he then called to young Ron Simington, "I'll take a turn at the wheel. Come on down and give Zeke a hand."

Soberly old Zeke went to work, and soon a silent and equally sober Ron Simington was beside him, just as busy.

Meanwhile Steve Argyle made his way forward on the pitching craft, climbed the fo'castle steps beside the mast, and made his way into the wheelhouse. There, his hands on the lashed wheel, he peered through the water-streaked windows of the wheelhouse at the other boats.

Still they appeared motionless. As far as he could tell, both distant skippers intended to ride out the blow and keep on fishing.

But outside, the white-capped waves were high, and the wind was lashing sea foam into a torrential, horizontal storm that was soaking his two hands as they labored at the stern.

Quickly he rigged the signal lantern and, topside in the wind but bracing himself against the low railing, he began signalling the other ships, asking their intentions. Just as quickly the responses from both came back, and as Steve Argyle reentered the wheelhouse he felt a little foolish. They were staying, both of them, and the tone of both their messages let him know instantly that they considered this just another blow that they would ride out with ease.

Yet he couldn't assuage his feeling that something was terribly wrong—wrong and rapidly getting worse. So, what should he do?

"Heavenly Father," he prayed as he bowed his head, "am I being warned by thee? Do we need to make a run for it? I want to stay at least until we can reel in, because I can't afford to replace my lines and gear, and both my hands feel we should remain that long, as well. But I have this awful feeling—"

Suddenly Steve Argyle's mind was filled with the memory of a phrase he had heard a few Sundays before, during a class lesson at the tiny LDS branch he and his family attended. He could not even remember the topic of the lesson, but the phrase "a stupor of thought" now filled his mind.

"A stupor of thought," the instructor had said, "is a feeling of mental numbness when a decision can't be reached in comfort. It is a nagging by the Holy Ghost to let you know that what you are contemplating and have prayed about is incorrect. It is a worrisome, empty feeling that will not go away until you acknowledge it and respond by changing your will to fit the will of God.

"A stupor of thought is a divine warning to the prayerful person."

His eyes still closed, Steve Argyle once again prayed fervently. "Heavenly Father, if I have been having a stupor of thought, then please help me to know what to do—"

And then abruptly he stopped, his eyes wide open, his mind filled with the certain understanding that he was going about this prayer of his all wrong.

"No," he prayed again, his voice resolute, "that is the wrong way to approach this, Heavenly Father, and I am sorry. I need to make the decision and then seek a confirmation instead of leaving the decision to thee.

"So, Heavenly Father, here is my decision. I am certain this has been a stupor of thought I have been feeling! Therefore, I am being told that we need to leave, and now. To do so, we shall cut the lines and make a run for it.

"Dear Father, wilt thou now give me peace in this decision I have made."

Moments later, as Steve Argyle fought his way aft across the slippery, heaving deck, a sharp knife in his hand, both Zeke and Ron wiped the spray from their faces and looked upon him with a mixture of surprise and relief.

"I hope you don't mind, lads," Steve Argyle shouted as he stepped to and swung the razor-edged knife, instantly severing the taut stern line. "But I've a feeling that we need to be running, and now! Lines and gear can be replaced, but it's not so easy to replace a good boat, or a good crew, either one.

"Zeke, take this knife and finish the task with the other lines, both port and starboard. Ron, my lad, raise the boom, secure the fishing poles, and batten down the hatches. I'll be topside in the wheelhouse, with the engine running full. Before ever we reach Kachamak Bay, lads, I've a feeling we'll be having us a gale, maybe the likes of which none of us have ever seen."

As old Zeke took the knife from the skipper, he nodded with satisfaction. Then, as Steve Argyle scuttled forward across the slippery deck, now awash with boarding seas, toward the fo'castle ladder, Zeke grabbed the coat front of his young companion.

"Ron, me lad," he shouted against the growing background of howling wind, "did you see the skipper's clear eye? Moments ago he was doubtful and his eye was cloudy, but no more. No more, I tell ye! Somehow he threw a line upward to heaven and got the tugs just right when he reeled it back in.

It's time and past to be out of here, and the skipper can feel it."

"How do you know that, Zeke?" Ron Simington shouted, his confusion evident. "The other boats aren't leaving. How do you know he's right?"

"Because, me bucky," Zeke snarled, "this old salt can feel it, too. I tell ye, me boy, if we stick to that clean-shaven land-lubber skipper of ours like barnacles to a whale's belly, we'll weather ever storm 'twixt here and yonder. I have me a feelin' on that one, as well. He's got something we can all learn from, and I aim to find out what that something is!

"Now, heave to, lad, and let us be gone from this hellish sea!"

And less than an hour later, the storm had been born and was gusting in furiously against the small craft, which was running dark and rain-wet off the Kenai Peninsula. But at least she was running on the storm's front edge, and all three men aboard knew the strong throbbing of the engine would be able to thrust them to safety.

But while the *Ginnie Marie* was scuttling toward the haven of home port, the storm was whipping up the salt-chop across the Gulf of Alaska, tossing other craft about like paper toys, and moving south, spinning with ever-increasing fury toward the south and southeast.

Truly a monster storm had been born.

Friday and Saturday,
October 28 and 29, 1910

The Pacific Northwest

By Friday, October 28, the low-pressure system in the Gulf of Alaska is well developed, and the squall line marching just before the cold front is headed south-southwest, pushed along by the prevailing westerlies and still following the deepening path of the polar jet stream. As the front moves, a succession of cloud formations appear before it, warning the wary that a storm is on the way. This actually becomes a miniature cold front and may develop as much as sixty miles ahead of the major front. These cloud formations, in the order they appear along the northern Canadian coast, are first, cirrus clouds; second, cumulus clouds; third, stratus clouds; and fourth, nimbus clouds. Last come the heavy winds and rains of the cumulonimbus, the squall line that precedes the cold front itself.

The first land damage done by this storm is to an Indian fishing village on Kunghit Island, southernmost of the Queen Charlotte Islands. But these native people have long known storms, as well as the clouds which reveal their coming. Thus, though the winds and pelting sleet flatten and destroy their casually erected shelters, the people themselves are long gone from the exposed village, and they weather the storm nicely in the lee of a sheltered bay far up the inner coast of Moresby Island.

By Saturday, October 29, the squall line has marched onward down Queen Charlotte Sound and has thoroughly buffeted both the Pacific Range of mountains on the mainland coast and Vancouver Island out in the Pacific. Although the air of the front has warmed slightly, and the snow and sleet of the day before are now reduced to blowing, torrential rains, there is still much destruction and danger.

Telephone and power lines are down in Nanimo; an electrical trolley in Victoria has blown over, injuring a number of people; several small fishing craft have been swamped north of Texada Island in the Strait of Georgia; and the ferry from Vancouver to Victoria has been forced to hold in port until the front has passed.

And at a lonely lighthouse northwest of Lasqueti Island—

UNDERSTANDING

The waves pounded against the lighthouse on Sisters Rock with an unrelenting fury—never lessening, always growing. A heavy overcast sky pressed low on the Strait of Georgia, and the mountain ranges on Vancouver Island to the west and Lasqueti Island directly behind to the southeast were shrouded from view by a thick, misty veil. Up from the waterfront, a mottled gray sea gull soared past the lighthouse window, its course a silent flight that seemed to the silently watching Merian Judson a hopeless gesture of effort in the face of overpowering odds. Moments later the gull was followed by several coots and then a black Siwash duck with its stumpy wings and brilliant yellow tail, all beating a path straight away from the coming storm.

And there was indeed a storm brewing—a wicked one, Merian thought—reckoned scientifically by the headlong drop of the aneroid barometer.

Anxiously the young man peered through the rain-streaked glass, doing his best to get an understanding of what he might be facing. Against the wind, the warning sound of the fog bell tolled constantly. Beside and behind him, the oil-fed wicks of the Argand Lamp burned brightly and smoke-lessly, radiating through the Fresnel catadioptric system of mirrors, lens, and prisms. The entire instrument was twelve feet high and weighed, because of all of the glass, upwards of five tons. Best of all, it could put out 80,000 to 100,000 candlepower of light in a continuous 360-degree horizontal beam, thus warning boats in all directions of the dangerous shoals and rocks upon which the lighthouse rested.

Merian Judson had studied that light, learning all he could about it during the last week in case something happened and he should be required to repair it. He hoped such an event would not occur, but in a storm like the one rising outside, it did not pay to take chances.

Again he strained to see out of the window. This was a real blow, with as heavy seas as he had ever seen in the Strait, and he was truly worried. Earlier the wind had blown hard from the west, and he had felt certain it was a Qualicum, a dangerous enough storm but usually localized to the Strait. However, he hadn't seen the usual blue-black streak on the gray of the ocean, and that should have warned him.

A little later the wind had abruptly shifted and was now howling directly down the Strait out of the northwest and the Queen Charlotte Sound. It was lashing and churning the sea, throwing spray and spume as high as his lighthouse window, almost drowning the lonely sound of the tolling fog bell outside.

Merian also should have noticed the warning clouds and the too-light colored sea and therefore better prepared his family. But he hadn't done much more than secure the shutters on the tender's house windows, and now it was almost as if—

"Merian?"

Turning, Merian glanced at his wife, Harriet, who was standing on the lighthouse stairs so that only her head was above floor level.

"Merian, the girls are getting frightened."

"I don't blame them," Merian Judson responded quietly. "This is getting nasty. I think winter has come early this year, and come with a vengeance."

"Will we . . . will we be all right, do you think?"

"Certainly," he said, forcing a calm into his voice that he didn't really feel. "We'll be fine. I'm worried more about the light. If it should go out for some reason, I don't know if I could get it relit. Harry told me it was quite a process, and from what I can learn, he was right. I've been studying it out, though, and I think I could do it. The trouble is, it would take time, and what if there were a ship out there?

"Besides," Merian continued as he looked anxiously up the Strait, "I haven't seen Jimmie Riddell yet, and I know he took the *Quit* up early last night."

For a long moment he stared into the storm, thinking of the man called Jimmie Riddell. He was a funny man, that one, and just different enough to keep most folks off balance with his unique humor. But he was also a fisherman, and a good one, being one of the best gill netters in the islands.

In his mind Merian pictured the *Quit*, its bow high and its stern so low with the weight of the gill net that it didn't appear to be there at all. He also thought of how Jimmie fished, all alone, stringing the net out until it stood in the sea like a tennis net across a court, a web nine hundred feet long and twenty feet deep, its upper edge held afloat by corks, its lower sunk by lead weights spaced close together. The outer end of his net was buoyed to a float which carried a flag and a lantern; the inner, to the bitts of the *Quit*. Thus set—and set in the evening, since even dog salmon can only be taken by gills in the dark—Jimmie, his boat, and his net drifted with the changing tides until dawn. Then he hauled in his catch— ten salmon, a hundred, or perhaps none, his web having been torn by sharks or fouled heavy with worthless fish.

It was hard work, and brutal, and Jimmie was always threatening that the next time he got a little money he would buy a bigger craft and go to purse seining. That, he had told Merian time and time again, was the real way to fish. Simply play the seine out over a roller on a revolving platform aft. Then steer the vessel slowly in a sweeping circle as the net went out, a circle perhaps a thousand feet in diameter. Then, when the circle was complete, the two ends of the net would have met at the seiner's stern. A power winch next hauled on ropes and the net closed, letting nothing escape. Instead it drew together until it was a bag, a "purse" drawn up under the vessel's counter, full of glistening fish.

"A thousand salmon at a haul is nothing," Jimmie would boast whenever he would warm to his subject. "Three thousand is common, and five thousand is far below the record. Why, purse seines have been burst wide open by the sheer weight of the fish against the pull of the winch! Yes, sir,

Merian, one of these days I'll be rid of the *Quit* for good, and then I'll be bringing in some real catches."

Again Merian peered out into the storm, worried for the man who had been such a good friend since he and Hattie had moved to the island to rear their growing family.

"Mercy," he said then as he shook his head, "what a week to spell off Harry Higgins and his wife!"

"But Harry didn't know the storm was coming."

Spinning in surprise, Merian looked down at where his wife was standing, watching him. He had been so caught up in worrying about Jimmie Riddell that he had forgotten entirely that she was standing on the stairs, awaiting his instructions.

"I know he didn't, Hattie," Merian finally replied. "But this storm is big, and I am so afraid that something will go wrong. I wish I knew a little more about lighthouses, or about what to do if something happened."

"I . . . I wish you did, too."

Now Merian looked closely at his wife, his voice revealing both his hesitancy and his concern. "Do you . . . want me to join you and the girls?"

Slowly Hattie looked away. "I . . . don't know if it would help, Merian. Beatrice is already terrified enough—"

"What is it going to take, Hattie?" Merian interrupted, frustration evident in his voice. "How can I convince Beatrice that she doesn't need to be afraid of me?"

"You might try speaking gently with her," Hattie replied. "When you speak to her, your voice is always so harsh and stern. Beatrice thinks that you dislike her."

"That's foolish. I just can't abide her disobedience, and I don't think we ought to kowtow to it."

"Merian, being gentle isn't kowtowing to anything! Besides, that little child doesn't have a disobedient bone in her body. She is a dreamer, a child of great imagination, and she just gets so engrossed in her dreams that she either doesn't hear us or else forgets. But as for deliberately disobeying? Never!"

"Well, maybe I can't abide dreamers. It seems to me that dreaming is a mighty foolish waste of time."

Hattie smiled. "Where do you want to be living next year?" she then asked, apparently changing the subject.

"What does that have to do with anything?"

"Just answer the question, M. J."

Merian shrugged. "The Point on Lasqueti, Hattie, in that nice home. We've talked of it often enough that you had ought to know."

"And wouldn't you call that a dream, Merian?"

Merian blinked as he looked at his wife. "I . . . uh . . . that is a plan, Hattie, and a plan is different from a dream. Without plans, we would wander aimlessly through life."

Hattie smiled again. "I agree. But, Merian, a plan is never made without an underlying dream. How do you know that Beatrice is not simply preparing, by dreaming, to lay plans for a glorious future?"

Merian started to answer, sputtered a little, and finally grinned at his wife. "All right," he said with a shrug, "I concede. She can dream if she wants." Then he turned back to the window, where the salt spray was obscuring everything. "But that isn't what we are speaking of, Hattie. Our problem is that Bea has become afraid of me, and I don't know how to get her back again."

"Gentleness in your voice would help."

"I know. And I'm surely trying to do better. But it will take more than that, I know it will. I've prayed about it for weeks, ever since I realized how she was feeling. But nothing comes, and I really don't know what to do."

"Mommy?"

"What is it, Freda?" Hattie Judson turned back down the stairs, and in a brief lull in the wind, Merian became aware of the faint sounds of children crying.

"Mommy, I can't get Beatrice to stop whining, and baby Lucy must be sick. She's been crying for the longest time now, and she won't stop, either."

With quick, nervous steps, Hattie descended the lantern-lit stairs, and once again Merian was alone. Faintly, from below, he could hear the sounds of his wife and daughters. They were no longer crying but were now singing "Merry Little Leapfrog John," a nonsense song that Hattie called her happy song. She sang it whenever the children were sad or frightened, and Merian smiled as he thought of how well it worked.

Hattie was quite a woman, he reflected. She was always nervous about new or threatening things, and yet she was filled with a sort of pioneer courage that carried her through all sorts of troubles and danger, allowing her to walk, as it might be said, where angels feared to tread.

Now, if only he could think of a way to get back in step

with her in nurturing the children, especially in terms of his doe-eyed, constantly dreaming second daughter.

Another gust howled past the lighthouse tower, and Merian turned and strode to the system of chains and weights that ran the fog bell. Pulling the weights up, he wound the bell so that it would continue tolling for the next twenty-four hours. Then he stepped again to the windows.

Off to the east, not more than a mile away, the Finnerty Islands, known locally as the Flat Tops because of their geographical formation, had completely vanished in the storm. Even the other two rocks that made up the Sisters group were invisible in the soupy mist.

Merian stood, peering outward, trying to see beyond the sea spray and the fog, thinking of winter days on Lasqueti when the fog would creep in and the cries of the gulls and the loons would combine with the whistling of squaw duck wings, making him shiver with loneliness. Now, with the banshee howling of the nor'wester pounding against the wooden structure around him, he suddenly felt lonelier than ever.

How he ached for the missing Jimmie Riddell! The *Quit* was a sound little craft, but in a gale such as this there was no telling what might happen. If Jimmie had found a cove somewhere along Vancouver Island to the lee of the wind, he would be just fine. But if this thing had caught him on the open sea . . .

"Hattie," he called anxiously as he turned back to the dimly lit stairs, "how are the girls?"

"Frightened," his wife called back. "Should . . . should I bring them up there, do you think?"

Merian looked around, thinking about his wife's question. Would it help them to be up there with him? he wondered. Or would Beatrice's obvious fear of him, which she showed whenever he spoke to her or came near her, compound the natural fright that the storm was bringing out in all of them?

"No," he finally answered as he felt the tower shudder with the force of the wind, "I don't think so. Uh . . . I'll come down, Hattie, and we'll take them into the tender's house together."

"But the walkway, Merian. Is it safe? This wind is strong enough to sweep us right off it. And if one of these seas should come across the rock—"

"Hattie, the lighthouse is too exposed, and too cold, for us to stay here much longer. Every gust shakes it right down to the pilings, the temperature is dropping by the minute, and I don't blame the girls for being frightened. Now, if I come with you, and if we all cling to each other as well as to the railing, we should be just fine."

"Oh, Merian, are you certain?"

"Well, I hope so. In the house we can at least have a fire, and there is food there, as well. Now, get the girls ready, and I'll be down directly."

Quickly Merian checked the weights for both the bell and the revolving light. All looked good, as did the level of oil in the reservoir for the lamps. After a quick walk around the room to recheck the sealing of the windows, he turned and started down the stairs, closing the trap door in the floor as he descended.

In the gloom of the small round room he made out the form of his wife, standing with little Beatrice snuggled in her arms. Feeling a stab of emotional pain that he had inadvertently caused his child to fear him, Merian stooped and took little Lucy into his arms. Then, taking six-year-old Freda by the hand, he opened the lower trapdoor, took a quick breath as the frigid, spray-filled air whipped up at him, and then quickly descended the wet, slick stairs through the open pilings that supported the lighthouse, pulling his eldest daughter behind him.

Once on the ground he grasped the iron railing that followed the wooden walkway to the tender's house, got Freda in front of him, and then set himself so that little Lucy's face was covered as much as possible by his coat.

"Hattie," he shouted as he felt his wife bump into his back, "get in front of me!"

With an effort she did so, both of them now feeling the full power of the wind. It was driving straight against them, forcing them into the iron railing, and Merian hoped the metal was embedded deeply enough into the rock to support their combined weight.

The air was also filled with salt spray and rain, so thick that they could hardly breathe, let alone see more than a foot or so to the front. Yet the wooden walkway was still there, as was the iron railing.

"You ready?" Merian shouted.

"Yes!"

"Then let's go," he cried with a slight shove, and together he and his wife began inching along the wooden walkway, doing their best to get their small family to the safety of the small home that stood somewhere before them in the wet fury.

For the most part during that brief but terrifying journey Merian didn't think of much. But once, as he lifted his eyes, his gaze rested upon the face of little Beatrice, inches from his own, as she huddled with eyes squeezed closed against her mother's shoulder and neck.

How beautiful she was, Merian thought then. Beautiful, but so unlike what he had always thought a little child should be. Could Hattie be right, though? Could Beatrice's dreaming be simply the laying of plans for a glorious though still hidden future? Merian didn't know, but with God's help he would try to be more gentle.

"Hattie!" he shouted as he felt his wife suddenly slipping in front of him, "hold to the rod!"

Hattie Judson instantly took hold of the metal railing again, reestablished her footing, and began moving forward. But Merian, pushing from behind, was thinking a new thought about the iron railing they were clinging to. How odd that he would call it that—a rod, like the one ancient Nephi and his father Lehi had seen in vision.

In actual time the dash took hardly more than a minute, yet the spray and rain were spitting in across the strait through the bared teeth of the howling gale with such force that by the time Merian Judson and his family were inside the comfortable wooden structure and the door was battened behind them, all were soaked to the skin and shivering violently.

"Freda," he said quickly, barking orders like the ship's captain he had once dreamed of being, "help Bea off with her clothes. Hattie, snuggle little Lucy up in some blankets, and then fix us something to drink. I'll build a fire and get a little heat in here, and we'll warm up that drink of yours, too."

"That sounds wonderful," Hattie said with a quick smile as she went to work. "Thank goodness you thought to batten the shutters this morning."

"I'll say," Merian replied somberly as he piled some driftwood into the stone fireplace. "It's nice to know I did something right."

Carefully Merian started the fire and fanned the tiny flame, his thoughts a jumble of worries. In his mind he worked his way back around the house, securing the heavy wooden shutters over each of the windows on the main level.

He had also done the same thing with the upper windows, securing the shutters so that the force of wind and water would not shatter the glass. Now, as he mentally reviewed his efforts, he felt confident that all would hold through the storm.

But he did not feel such confidence in his efforts with his second daughter, his little dreamer. There he had failed, and he was not at all certain that he would ever be able to regain the child's confidence.

The other issue that continued to play in his mind was the issue of the iron rod, the word of God. Was that significant for him? he wondered. Might the Lord be giving him some sort of message in response to his prayers, a message that provided the answer as to how he might regain the trust of his little daughter?

Heavenly Father, he prayed mentally as he worked on the fire, *if thou art attempting to teach me, please make it more clear. If I am to think of thy word, then help me to know which words I need most. I don't . . . I . . .*

Merian slowly stopped praying, his attention arrested by a mental image of Jesus seated on a rock in ancient Palestine, with dozens of little children on his lap and clambering joyfully about. "Suffer little children to come unto me, and forbid them not: for of such is the kingdom of God," the Savior was saying, and for the first time in his life, Merian was actually considering the implications of that scripture.

"Suffer," the Savior had said, "and forbid them not." Might that mean to "allow under difficult circumstances?" Might Christ then be saying to Merian, "Suffer Beatrice to be a dreamer, Merian. Don't forbid her this gift, for though it is difficult for you to tolerate, such pure dreamers find place in the kingdom of heaven."

Startled by the thought, Merian sat back on the rug. *Heavenly Father,* he thought, *is this thy word that thou hast been wanting me to consider?*

As a sweet warmth filled his being, another thought entered Merian's mind—a thought as surprising as the first. *Maybe,* he found himself thinking, *if he could somehow learn to dream with little Beatrice . . .*

Later, wearing dry clothes and nursing the flames in the small setback fireplace into a warm fire, Merian turned to see his two eldest daughters wrapped in blankets and standing silently behind him, their teeth chattering with the chill.

"You two look like Indians," he declared, forcing himself to smile. Instantly Beatrice took a step backward, and then another, but Merian fought back the feelings of anger, hurt, and despair that instantly filled his heart. Then, with great resolution, he plunged ahead.

"Did . . . did I ever tell you about the time, down in Utah, when an Indian brave got the drop on me . . . with his gun?"

Wide-eyed, Freda shook her head, though Beatrice did not respond. "Wh . . . what happened?" Freda whispered through chattering teeth.

"Well," Merian replied, turning so that he could face them and settling himself on the hearth rug, "I wanted to marry your mother, and so, it seems, did he."

"An *Indian* wanted to marry Mommy?" Freda asked in disbelief as she seated herself on her father's lap. "A real live Indian?"

"He certainly did, and I can't say that I blame him. But when I told him it was no good and that I was going to marry her instead, he pulled out his gun and stuck it in my ribs."

"What happened then?" Freda asked breathlessly.

"What happened?" Merian continued, his face serious, his eyes never leaving Beatrice's. "Well, I tried to take his gun away from him, and he shot me. I died, and that old Indian married your mother."

"Did he really?" Beatrice finally asked, not noticing at all the look of dismay and disgust her older sister was giving her father. "Did . . . you go to heaven?"

"Daddy," Freda fumed, "that wasn't true, and you should be ashamed of yourself for telling it. And he didn't go to heaven, Bea, because he didn't even die!"

"Freda's right," Harriet Judson said quietly, as she handed her husband a cup of warm broth. "Merian, if you are going to teach our daughters with stories, then they ought to be truthful ones."

Merian laughed innocently. "Aw, Hattie, I was only funning, trying to dream with Beatrice, if you will, and there can't be any harm in that. You said so yourself. Besides, that old Indian back in Utah . . ."

Suddenly the house was filled with a terrible roaring, and a terrific gust of wind and water shook the wooden structure of the tender's home clear to its deeply embedded foundation. Seconds later another blast of wind and heaving wave beat across the rock and into the side of the small, framed home, and instantly both older girls fled to their mother in tears.

"Hush," Harriet scolded gently as she comforted them and little Lucy. "We'll be fine, girls. We just need to exercise faith, and the Lord will see us through."

"That he will," Merian added quietly.

"Do you have another story, Merian?"

Merian Judson looked up at his wife. "A dream story, Hattie?"

Slowly Hattie nodded. "Yes, Merian. A dream story—about faith. I've a feeling we all need to lay some plans in that direction."

For a long moment Merian stared into the fire. Then he turned and held out his arms to his three daughters. Freda came willingly, and Hattie placed Lucy in Merian's arms. But still Beatrice held back, clinging uncertainly to her mother.

With a look of pain in his eyes such as Hattie had never seen, Merian dropped his arm. "I do have another story," he declared quietly. "And this is a true story, about faith, just like your mother wanted. Do you girls have faith that the Lord can protect us from this awful weather?"

Freda nodded soberly, though still Beatrice said nothing.

"That's good, Freda. Now, don't waver in your faith, no matter how noisy the storm gets. If you waver, maybe God can't protect you anymore. That's what once happened to me.

"It was down in Darington, in Washington," Merian continued. "Your Uncle Fred and I had taken a job building a railroad, and I had been given the tools and the job of making railway ties.

"One day a fire broke out near my ties. It was Sunday, and I could see that the fire would burn itself out before it did any kind of real damage. So I would not go over with the others to fight it. I wanted to keep that day holy, and fighting a fire that was not threatening anything but a few ties and tools did not seem like a good way to do it. Besides, I had faith to believe that my newly cut ties would not burn, which worked out fine until just before dark. Then I walked over to see how things were. There my ties were, not harmed at all, though the fire had burned all around them. It was the same with my tools. In spite of the fact that the fire had burned all around them, my tools had not been harmed.

"Well, had I turned and gone back to camp right then, those ties and tools of mine would have been safe. But, girls, I weakened just a little. I picked up my tools and threw them over in a damp spot, 'just in case.' Then I turned to go back to camp.

"I had not gone very far, however, when my ties and tools were all ablaze. My faith had weakened, just as Peter's had when he tried to walk on the water, and I had lost. Otherwise I would have been completely protected by the Lord."

Merian ceased, and Harriet looked at her daughters. "That, dears, is a true story. Now, we have prayed and asked to be protected, and we must have faith, or believe, that we *will* be protected. Can you exercise faith with your father and me?"

Again Freda nodded. And again, Beatrice did not respond. "Beatrice?"

Slowly the small child looked up at her mother. "Does Heavenly Father have faith?" she asked quietly.

"Of course he does. Heavenly Father has perfect faith."

"Then Daddy doesn't have faith."

While Merian looked on in surprise, Hattie knelt beside her young daughter. "Of course Daddy has faith, Beatrice. He just didn't have enough faith that one particular day. But now he's learned his lesson."

For a moment Beatrice pondered her mother's words. Then, at last, she spoke again. "Is the storm Heavenly Father's way of being angry with us?"

Surprised, Merian and Hattie looked at each other, hardly knowing how to respond.

"Beatrice," Merian finally said, "a storm is just a storm, a noisy way for Heavenly Father to send water down to earth. He isn't angry with us and would never show anger by making little children like you suffer in a storm. He loves us and always wants to help us and be kind to us."

"Then why is Daddy always angry at me?" Beatrice asked as she looked up at her mother. "If he has faith like Heavenly Father, why doesn't he love me?"

Dumbfounded, Merian and Hattie simply stared at each other. Then, as the banshee howling of another furious windburst shrieked past the house, filling the terrible silence of the room with a horrid, almost unheard noise, Merian Judson slowly rose to his knees in the attitude of prayer.

Quickly Hattie kneeled facing her husband, while little Beatrice stood resolutely beside her.

"Oh, dear God in heaven," Merian began as huge tears of pain and sorrow welled up in his eyes. "I . . . I have offended one of these, thy innocent ones, and I do not know how to tell her how terribly sorry I am."

Furiously the storm raged, both without and within, as the wind and water fought to break in and Merian fought to control his sorrow and his emotions. Then, haltingly, he opened his heart to heaven, and his family listened in quiet attention as he spoke of his own youthful hopes and dreams —of a wife that would love him always, of a family that would grow closer together eternally, and of a home of their own where they would enjoy safety and security. He spoke too of his frustrations that times were so difficult economically and that he was so constantly unemployed that even this one-week job was a cherished opportunity. Finally he spoke once again of his sorrow that he had offended his precious little daughter, who had come from heaven with gifts that he had simply not understood.

"Dear Father," he pleaded as tears coursed down his face, "I do not know what to do. Touch my heart so that it will be made as soft and gentle as thy own love. Grant me the faith to know that such a love can be mine. But above all, please . . . please, in the name of the Master of love, even Jesus Christ, our Savior, please touch the heart of little Beatrice. Suffer her to come unto me, that in time she might let me love her once again."

With that fervent plea, Merian could say no more; with tears falling freely, he sank back to a sitting position on the large braided rug that lay before the fire.

Hattie, her own heart breaking and her own tears joining those of her husband, was wondering what to do next when she felt little Beatrice pull away from her.

Wiping her eyes and looking up, Hattie watched as the little four-year-old stepped slowly to the side of her weeping father. For a moment she stood as if in deep thought. And then, still moving slowly, almost shyly, she lifted his hand and arm and settled in under them, squirming next to him. Then, gently, she took the corner of her blanket and began wiping her father's tear-streaked face.

At first Merian didn't respond. Then, slowly, as he real-ized what little Beatrice had done, he rose once again to his knees, holding his daughter tightly in his arms, and sent his voice heavenward.

Moments later, with the little family all huddled closely to-gether before the fire, a beaming Hattie finally spoke. "We should thank Heavenly Father for this storm, M. J."

"I have," Merian replied softly as he swiped once again at his misty eyes.

"I'm glad," Hattie replied sweetly. "Now together, everybody, let's sing 'Merry Little Leapfrog John' one more time. Ready?"

They were, and soon the snug little house on Sisters Rock, north of Lasqueti Island in the Strait of Georgia, battered by the unseasonable winter storm, was filled with the sound of happy music.

But the storm raged on, beating south-southeast, bearing death and destruction—as well as life—upon its icy breath.

DAY FOUR

Sunday, October 30, 1910

Wenatchee, Washington

The cities of Wenatchee and Entiat lie to the lee of the Cascade Mountains and on the Columbia River Gorge, in central Washington. As the prevailing westerlies carry the storm inland along the shifting route of the polar jet stream, the cold front slams directly into the Cascades. Rising to get over these mountains, the air cools, releasing rain and then snow. Many times such moisture will fall only on the windward slopes, but for storms as massive as the one we have been following, moisture will continue to fall even after the front pushes across the crest of the mountains.

To add to the storm's continuing ferocity, the cold air of the front picks up renewed speed as it slides down the eastern slopes of the mountains, generating even higher winds. Also, warm air is once again tumbled ahead of this rush of cold air in the bulldozer effect, more monster cumulonimbus clouds are formed, and the squall line that swept down the northwest coast is now enhanced and enlarged, dumping more moisture than ever.

On Sunday, October 30, this massive wave of energy slides into the Columbian River Gorge, where, among other things, the high winds and spitting snow capsize the Entiat Ferry and raise other havoc up and down the river.

And in a home located about equal distance between Wenatchee and Entiat—

COURAGEOUS CHRISTIANITY

The LDS Sunday School opening hymn had just concluded when the door of the George Benson home was thrown open and a man burst through. His clothing was Sundayish though disheveled, and his sheepskin overcoat carried a silver star that showed the white residue of the rapidly growing blizzard.

"Mister Oaks," he shouted before the small but startled congregation. "Excuse me, please, but is David Zeller here today?"

Branch President Merlin Oaks, a large and gentle man, whose beard was speckled with gray, rose to his feet. "I think I saw him, but—"

"He's here," Debbie Zeller stated as she rose to her feet. "He's back in the kitchen with one of the boys."

"Did I hear my name called?" David Zeller, a thin, balding young man who was known, in spite of his relative youth, as an expert river runner, strode into the room and halted at the sight of the county sheriff.

"You surely *did* hear your name called. Dave, we've got trouble. The storm has capsized the Entiat Ferry, and there are at least two people stranded on the rocks above the falls. You're the only man I know who has a chance of getting to them."

For a long moment David Zeller stood quietly, silent words passing between himself and his wife, Debbie. Both of them knew what was being asked of him, and both of them felt the tight hand of fear clutch at their very souls. Boating in the rapids beneath where the ferry ran was dangerous enough in the best of conditions, but in a killer storm such as this was becoming, there was a good chance that a man would never return.

Then, with a resolution born of knowing what was right, Debbie smiled her incredibly bright smile, her eyes flashed, and the dimple on her left cheek, the dimple that more than anything else had made David first notice her and want to love her, puckered in and held.

"Of course he'll go," Debbie declared brightly. "In fact, we'll both go."

"Do you need help?" President Oaks asked quietly, his gaze resting on David Zeller.

"I will," David responded as his mind began to organize

the rescue operation. "For what has to be done, I think I'd be best off using a canoe. Debbie and I will pick mine up and meet you there. As far as what I need on shore, I want a tent set up, a good-sized one, and several fires built in a circle out in front of it. Then, of course, we'll want plenty of blankets and dry clothing, and some hot broth. And, Sheriff, do you have that gun handy, the one that shoots a line?"

"I'll get it."

"Good. I'll need it, because I can't drag a rope through that stretch of the Columbia. Now, if I—"

"Say! Wait just a minute here!"

The outburst stunned them all into silence, and every face in the room turned toward the old man whose thin, high voice had just interrupted David Zeller.

"You have a problem, Brother Abe?" President Oaks asked, his voice hesitant.

"We *all* have a problem, President," Abe Jacobs stated indignantly. "This here is our Sunday worship service, which the Lord has commanded us to hold, and it ain't proper for this tin-horn gentile sheriff to come in here busting it up this way."

There was a rustle of voices, and for a moment President Merlin Oaks was too astonished to reply. Finally, however, he made the effort.

"Abe, uh . . . you're right, about the meeting, that is. We have been commanded to hold it. But we've . . . well, we've elected the sheriff here, and this is an emergency—"

"How do you know it's a real emergency?" Abe Jacobs demanded. "And even if it is, there's plenty of other folks who can help him out, folks that don't care two hoots about going to church. I still say he's got no call bustin' up our meeting this way! I came here to have a meeting, and by thunder I expect a meeting!"

"What about Christianity, Jacobs?" the sheriff asked, his own voice revealing indignation. "You claim to be Christian. Didn't Jesus teach that we were supposed to love our neighbors?"

"You're a fine one to preach Christianity, Sheriff," Abe snarled. "I know you pretty well, and you've got enough bad habits to stoke all the furnaces in hell."

"Probably so," the sheriff retorted. "But one of them isn't being a hypocrite. Zeller," he then said, abruptly dismissing old Abe Jacobs from his mind, "we're burning daylight. You ready to go?"

"I am."

"Anything else you need?"

"Yes," David replied absently while he looked out at the raging storm, and while Abe Jacobs muttered his disgust. "Lots of luck and blessings. And somebody had better bring a backup boat of some sort, just in case I don't make it."

Quietly the sheriff nodded, and President Oaks looked gravely at old Abe Jacobs.

"Brother Jacobs, I'm sorry to do this, but I am dismissing the meeting. The sheriff and Brother Zeller need our help, and they need it there at the river. Not here."

"You do that," Abe Jacobs responded angrily as David and Debbie Zeller ran out to their team and wagon, "and I'll file charges against you with the district presidency. I'll . . . I'll . . . ah, what's the doggone use anyway!"

President Oaks shrugged. "You do what you think you have to do, Brother Jacobs, because I'm going to do the same. Brothers and sisters, we will bring this meeting to a conclusion with prayer, which I will offer. When I am finished, please proceed as quickly as possible to gather the items Brother Zeller asked for. Then take them to the landing so we can set up everything as quickly as possible. Ralph, could you bring your boat as a backup?"

A man in the rear quickly nodded.

"Good. Now, let us pray. Dear Heavenly Father, in this our hour of need, we petition thee for wisdom and protection . . ." And shortly thereafter, the small North Wenatchee Branch of The Church of Jesus Christ of Latter-day Saints dispersed early.

A little more than an hour later, as a crowd of mostly LDS people scrambled to set up a rescue base on the bank of the mighty Columbia River, just below the tiny farming village of Entiat, a bundled-up Debbie Zeller stood close to her husband. The snow was falling heavily, but it was the wind that was making conditions so bad. The storm was practically horizontal, and except for occasional brief intervals, visibility was almost nonexistent.

"What do you suppose got into Abe Jacobs?" Debbie asked as she shivered with the cold and watched her husband ready his canoe.

"Who knows?" David answered as he adjusted his gloves. "Crazy, wasn't it?"

"It was certainly strange. But then, he's strange anyway, living all alone like he does. Did you know that he's down there now, with the rest of the branch? But he isn't helping any, I noticed that. He's just standing there, staring at the river."

"Well," David said as he straightened up, "it's obvious he has a problem of some sort. Listen, honey, I . . . I've got to go."

"I love you," Debbie whispered as she pulled her husband close to her and kissed him.

"Thank goodness," David smiled in reply. "If you didn't, I probably wouldn't even try to come back. I'd just keep floating down that crazy old river."

Debbie smiled, thinking of how she loved this man, this skinny fellow with the big gap between his front teeth that gave him the happiest smile she had ever seen. Occasionally, the gap made him whistle his words, but he could also squirt through it a stream of water, often as far as twenty feet, and he delighted the children in the neighborhood by doing that. He would do the same for their own children, too. Debbie knew that. He would, just as soon as they were able to have some—

"It's time, sweet," David said, interrupting her thoughts. "Take the wagon back downstream to the camp, and tell the sheriff to keep those fires up. The flames may be all I will be able to see through this mess. Tell him also that I will empty my pistol into the air once I get to the rocks, and before I fire off the rope. That way the people on shore will have a chance to get behind wagons or something so they won't get hit."

Debbie nodded, and without another word David turned and launched his loaded canoe into the turbulent and storm-ravaged river.

The next twenty minutes were filled with agony for Debbie and all the others who waited on shore. Once or twice the wind slowed and they could dimly see David's tiny craft being tossed wildly on the massive river. But usually all they could see was snow, and so the suspense was almost unbearable.

"Oaks," the sheriff finally said as he and the branch president stood there waiting, "you have no idea how I appreciate the help you and your folks are giving me."

"Well," President Oaks replied with a grin, "as you said, a little Christian service never harmed any Christian, so far as I have been able to learn. Even if it had to be rendered on a Sunday."

The sheriff smiled in return. "You're all right, Oaks."

"I . . . I'm sorry about old Abe Jacobs," Merlin Oaks apologized then. "He's a good man. He truly is! I just can't explain what got into him."

The sheriff shrugged his shoulders. "It takes all sorts, Oaks, and in this job I've seen 'em all, too. Guess it's a good thing I'm thick skinned, because I'm not too bothered by what he said. But one thing I've learned—even the least little thing can put a burr under a fellow's saddle. Big or little, it doesn't seem to matter. But once that burr is there, then Katie bar the door!"

President Oaks laughed softly. "Yeah, Sheriff, I'm learning the same thing. Is there anything else my people can do?"

"Just wait and keep on praying," the sheriff replied with a wry smile. "Oh, and one more thing. One of these days I'd like to learn a little more about the things you believe. There's something different about most of you people, Oaks, something that I'd like to understand."

As the sheriff walked away, Merlin Oaks pondered his words about burrs under folks' saddles. Well, something had put a burr under Abe Jacob's saddle, that was sure. Something had surely caused the man to react as he had to having the Sunday School meeting cancelled. But what could it have been, and how could he possibly help this fellow Latter-day Saint to extract that burr?

"Abe," he asked a few moments later as he walked over to stand beside the lonely-looking old man, "how can I help you?"

"Help me?" the man whined as he stared straight ahead. "It's a little late for that, President. Now let's just hope it ain't too late for that sorry fool Zeller, out there in his canoe."

Quizzically, President Oaks looked down at the older man —his stern visage, ramrod-straight posture, and incongruously cloudy eyes. Well, like the sheriff had said, a burr had surely worked itself under Abe Jacob's saddle somewhere. Now didn't seem to be the time or place to try to dig it out, but something made President Oaks open his mouth again.

"Abe, you ever been on the river in a storm?" he heard himself asking, even when he had intended all along to drop his feeble attempt at a conversation and walk away.

The older man nodded.

"Bad one?" the branch president continued, still surprised that he was standing there speaking with the older member of the Church. "Like this?"

"Worse, maybe."

Merlin Oaks was surprised. "That must have been some storm, Abe."

"It was. Worst storm of 1898."

"Dangerous?"

"I should hope to snort! Thirteen people died on this river in less time than it takes to tell it. Boat capsized just like that ferry, and they . . . they were all dead. *Thirteen*, President, including . . . my . . . wife and my daughter."

In dumbfounded silence, President Merlin Oaks stared at old Abe Jacobs. "So you know, don't you?" he said at last, his voice soft with understanding.

Silently the old man nodded.

"And back there at George Benson's, it wasn't the meeting at all."

Stubbornly the old man stared ahead. But abruptly his voice softened, and a torrent of words flowed forth, revealing the depth of his emotion and pain.

"I been a'watching those two Zeller kids ever since they was little," Abe stated quietly. "Watching, without either of them knowing I was doing it. Even afore she was married, Debbie Zeller put me in mind of my little daughter. Now that she's married to David, it's more than that. Now the both of them put me in mind of my wife and me, the way they carry on. Why, they even look at each other like we did! It's like . . .

"Well, anyhow, when that durn fool sheriff came in, asking for David to go out on that murderous river, it all came back to me, the horror of that day back in '98. That's when I knew I had to try and keep him off that water. If I didn't, then little Debbie'd be left alone just like I was.

"Well, that's been hell for me, President, that being alone. I wake up thinking my wife's beside me and she isn't; I'll hear the floor creak and before I know what I'm doing I'll call her name; and so on. It never seems to stop. Every day of my life I miss her. I probably ought to get married again, but I can't seem to work up enough interest to get the job done. But it has left me an empty old man, empty with nothing to fill the void but the Church.

"And then one day I noticed little Debbie, and the hole in my life started to get a little something pumped back in it."

With a loud *whumph* old Abe blew his nose into a red neckerchief he pulled out of his pocket. "So," he said as he got himself back under composure, "she and that husband of hers mean a whole lot to me. They don't know it, but they do!

That's why I jumped up today and started yelling the first fool thing that came to mind."

"It was a courageous thing to do," President Oaks stated gently.

"It was a fool thing to do! I hoped it would work, but . . . but, oh, dear Lord," the old man went on slowly as he broke into open sobs, "it didn't! I couldn't get the job done, and now the river'll get poor David just like it got my own family."

"Abe, you've got to have faith."

"That's mighty easy to say, President. I had faith back in '98, and look what it got me!"

"But you can't just give up. Here, let me get Debbie Zeller over here. Maybe if she knew how you felt, the two of you together—"

But old Abe Jacobs rose up fiercely. "No you don't, President! I don't want you telling her *or* her husband how I feel! I ain't about to let you make me into somebody's burden. Agreed?"

"But, Abe—"

"Doggone it, President, I mean it!"

President Oaks sighed with resignation. "All right, Abe. If you say so—"

"Sheriff," a man suddenly shouted from down near the river, interrupting the intense conversation between Abe Jacobs and President Oaks, "I just saw Dave Zeller. He's nearly at the rocks."

"I saw him, too," a woman shouted urgently. "But I think he's in trouble. The river's taking him into the rocks too fast, and he was paddling upstream for all he was worth. President Oaks, do you think—"

"I do," the big man declared, reading the woman's thoughts. "Folks, Brother David's in need of our faith right now. If you brethren would remove your hats . . ."

Startled, the sheriff removed his own hat as the men around him instantly did the same. President Oaks's wife, Sunny, walked to Debbie Zeller's side, and with a comforting smile took hold of her hand. And then President Merlin Oaks, who looked more like a prize fighter than the spiritual giant he was, bowed his head in prayer.

It was not a long prayer, nor was it flowery. Instead, the sheriff noted, it was a simple statement of the circumstances, and a plea for divine intervention in behalf of David and the people on the rocks who needed him so badly. Interestingly, it was also a prayer for Abe Jacobs and the rest of those on shore, that they might do well their part in the drama being played out around them.

The prayer was closed in the name of the Savior, there was an expectant hush, and then from across the water the sound of five revolver shots rang out.

"He's reached the rocks!" the sheriff cried, and then quickly he and Merlin Oaks huddled the people behind the wall of wagons that had been set up as a windbreak. Seconds later another report sounded above the shriek of the storm. Instantly the sound of a line whistled overhead, a man sprinted after it and hauled it back, and the sheriff quickly secured a heavy rope to the line. Then, after a series of tugs, the unseen David Zeller began hauling the heavy rope out across the river.

Anxiously the small crowd stood in the howling blizzard and watched as the sheriff played out the long line, careful that it did not twist or tangle. It was cold and miserable work, and the ferocity of the storm was incredible. Yet no one complained or murmured, and all stood silently in the open, trying to see through the snow to the unseen people out on the rocks.

Finally the line stopped, there was a long pause and then another series of tugs, and quickly the sheriff took the rope, wound it around a nearby tree, and secured it.

"All right," he shouted against the wind, "now, all we have to do is pull him in. Oaks, you take charge of that. Keep the pulling steady, not too fast, but we must be steady. You ladies, tromp a path in the snow back into the trees. We don't want these fellows slipping any more than they have to. And don't one of you stop your praying, even for a minute. If ever anyone needed our prayers, David Zeller and those folks with him are the ones.

"Now, are you all ready?"

Several men, the icy rope in their hands, nodded. Seeing that, the sheriff gave a final tug on the rope and was given an answering tug from somewhere out on the river.

"He's ready, men," he called softly. "Now, heave away!"

What followed was an agonizingly slow few minutes that Debbie Zeller would never forget for as long as she lived. Yet all seemed to be going well, until suddenly the rope went slack. Scramble as they would, the men could feel no pull on the rope, except that caused by the river, itself—and Debbie's heart nearly stopped with fear.

"Sheriff," President Oaks called in alarm, "I can't feel him!"

"No!" Debbie cried out. "Dear Heavenly Father, please don't let him die. He is such a good man."

"Are you sure, Oaks?" the sheriff shouted as he ran to the rope.

"Feel it yourself," President Oaks responded. "It's gone slack! Oh, dear God, please help them!"

"All of you," old Abe Jacobs suddenly screamed as he leaped forward, slid to a stop, and grabbed hold of the icy line, "run with the rope! Maybe he's hit a smooth stretch and is paddling faster than we can pull. Run, and catch up with him!"

"Run it, men!" President Oaks ordered in response. "Abe knows the river, and he knows what he's talking about. If you slip, let go and get out of the way! We've got some running to do!"

And run the men did, heavily through the snow, pulling the rope into the trees, dropping it, and scurrying back to the riverbank to grab up the icy, dripping line to begin running again. It was brutal, frigid work, and very quickly the mens' gloved but wet hands curled up with the cold so that they had little feeling left beyond the numbing chill. Yet no one slacked, no one complained, and above the din of their shouts and even the storm rang the constant, shrill voice of old Abe Jacobs, who would not quit.

"Feel anything yet?" the sheriff called urgently through the howling blizzard to a staggering Merlin Oaks.

"I . . . I don't," the branch president gasped. "If we could just get better footing, I'm sure . . ."

"President," old Abe Jacobs suddenly shouted as he picked up the rope on the bank and started to pull for his fourth or fifth turn, "I . . . I . . . we've got something out there!"

Instantly, President Oaks stopped running. "Good for you, Abe," he shouted with an urgent hope in his voice. "Now, slow it back down. If it's Brother Zeller, we don't want to capsize him. Steady, boys. Steady."

And steadily they pulled, until a short time later, in the midst of a swirling and furious attack of wind and snow, the bow of the canoe suddenly appeared and grated onto the gravel of the bank.

With a great shout, the sheriff, Merlin Oaks, and old Abe Jacobs were in the water, pulling the canoe around broadside to the bank. Then other hands were helping David Zeller, and surprisingly, two other men, a woman, and a small girl, all four nearly dead from exposure, up onto the shore.

Quickly they were lifted and carried to the warm area between the several large fires, and within seconds they were in dry clothing and wrapped in blankets under the shelter of the tent, while Debbie Zeller and the other women were forcing warm broth down their throats.

"Debbie," David Zeller asked a little later as they were loading the tiny canoe onto the wagon, preparing to follow President Oaks and the rescued people back toward Wenatchee. "You remember how old Abe Jacobs was acting earlier?"

"I do."

"He's still at it. Acting peculiar, I mean. He hasn't stopped looking at us ever since I got back. Have you noticed that?"

Debbie Zeller nodded. "I've noticed. I've been watching him myself. And he keeps crying, David. If he looks at us, or if he looks at that little girl you rescued, he breaks into tears. Do you suppose he's all right?"

"I don't know."

"Did . . . did you know it was him who kept the men on the rope when they thought they had lost you? Not only that, but he was probably pulling harder than anybody else there. It was an amazing thing to see."

David Zeller reached up and scratched his head. "Well, that beats all I ever heard. You just can't tell about some folks, can you? Say, Debbie, you don't suppose it would hurt to offer him a ride back into town with us, do you?"

With a bright smile Debbie Zeller shook her head. "Not hardly. Or invite him to Sunday dinner, either," she added quickly. Then, with flashing eyes and sweetly puckered dimple, she turned and walked toward the old man who had done so much to help her husband come back to her, the tender, lonely man she was getting ready to learn a great deal more about.

But the killer storm continued to sweep south and east, building and growing.

Monday, October 31, 1910

Vale, Oregon

As the cold front stretches out and moves southwest across the high, fertile lands of central Washington and the more arid country of eastern Oregon, all the time dropping gradually in elevation as it moves toward the Snake River Plain, the air once again warms slightly. There is still plenty of moisture being carried aloft, but as the cumulonimbus clouds roil and grow ahead of the front, the moisture no longer reaches the earth in the form of sleet and snow. Instead it appears as rain and hail.

And now another phenomenon appears in the massive clouds that are delivering the first terrific punches of this immense storm—thunder and lightning—and our clouds show off how they got their nickname, thunderheads.

These massive clouds, the tops of which may reach as high as twelve miles, contain violent ingredients such as tempest winds, fiercely swift updrafts and downdrafts, heavy rain, pelting hail, and lightning. It is common knowledge that lightning causes thunder, but a more difficult question might be, What causes lightning?

Electrically charged (ionized) ice crystals and water droplets within the wind-torn cumulonimbus are in constant, violent collision. In the same way that our bodies build up static electricity through friction with a carpet, this friction of electrically charged water particles causes the cloud to develop into something akin to a giant battery. The electrical charges then separate, with the positive charges accumulating near the top of the cloud and negative charges near the bottom.

Eventually, the cloud must release some of this electrical energy in the form of an electrical discharge—lightning. Such arcing of static electricity can happen within the same cloud, between two clouds, or between a cloud and the ground. Electricity thus shoots back and forth through the lightning channel several times within only a fraction of a second, and we see lightning.

The instantly following phenomenon, thunder, is caused by the intense heat surrounding the lightning channel. As the air close to the lightning bolt is instantly heated and forced to move very fast, it produces a sort of sonic boom—thunder. And in the storm we are following, all of this is accompanied by heavy precipitation.

As we watch, this all comes together on a small, lonely ranch, located somewhere to the southwest of the unsuspecting towns of Vale and Ontario, Oregon.

THE COMMITMENT

The new Mrs. Tamara Beecher looked anxiously at the sky. It was dark and lowering, and as the wagon bounced along the washboard of a road, she found herself worrying that her things in the wagon might get wet in the approaching storm.

Not that she wanted to go any faster. Goodness, no. In fact, they could have traveled much more slowly and she would have been happy. But the horses continued their steady gait, their hooves beating a distant-sounding thunder upon the road, and she knew with sinking heart that the inevitable was approaching. Soon they would be at her new husband's home, and she would in very fact become Brent Beecher's . . . *wife*. She thought of that, felt her stomach muscles tighten with apprehension, and with all her heart she tried to force both the thoughts and fears from her mind.

The wind was blowing now, fitful gusts that whipped the sparse grass of the eastern Oregon hills into a mad frenzy. Definitely a storm was building, and it had the look of a real gully washer. She was not frightened by that, but, strangely, she was truly frightened by the thoughts of being married, of living as a wife in her new husband's ranch home.

Husband. What a strange-sounding word that was! *Her* husband. Carefully, almost shyly, she glanced at the man who sat next to her on the spring seat, easily handling the skittish team of horses.

He was lanky and tall, six feet and seven inches, and she had never known a taller man. Besides that, and she grinned as she thought of it, he had the longest feet she had ever laid eyes upon. Size fifteens, he had told her. Helped him stay planted in the high Oregon winds, he had quipped the first time she had mentioned them.

And they had better, she thought, as she turned her back against the terrific gusts of cold air that were tearing at her new hat and coat. The wind was now more constant, and there was a low moan with it that sounded haunted, almost evil.

"Well," her husband drawled as he put his arm around her and drew her instantly stiffening form close to his side, "there's home."

She looked up and for the first time realized that they had crossed the low crest of a hill. Below them the small ranch was spread out, nestled in a U between three small hills. It was neatly arranged, tidy, and—to her surprise—quite pretty.

Except, that is, for the cabin.

As Brent pulled the team around and halted them before the low-roofed porch, the young bride's heart seemed almost to stop. The house was old and was nothing more than a log cabin, rough built at that. It was such a far cry from the lovely, spacious home of her youth back in Boise, and it was so terribly different from what she had expected, that she was stunned. How could she possibly live in *that?* How could Brent possibly expect her to become a woman in such a pitiful shack?

"Well, sweetheart, we're home. And from the way the clouds are churning across the point there, it's none too soon. Mercy, but this is turning into a real blow."

Silently she nodded. "It . . . it must be very windy up there."

"It is. All around us, in fact. That's one of the things I like about this little swale. Wind moans a lot, but down here it never slams into you like it does up on the hills. Oh, it tumbles around a little, but it never slams hard like it does up on top.

"Well, why don't I help you inside, and then I'll get the team and wagon put away."

Numbly Tamara nodded, extended her hand, and was helped graciously to the ground.

"Seems to me a new bride ought to be carried across her first threshold," Brent said quietly. "So . . ."

And without so much as a by-your-leave, the fiercely resisting Tamara was swept up into her husband's arms and carried through the door of the old log cabin.

"So, what do you think?" Brent Beecher asked as he turned her slowly around.

"Uh . . . ," she hesitated, her heart hammering with nervousness—and with a desire to get as far from this man as possible. "I . . . uh . . . Please put me down . . . so I can think. Then I . . . I'll tell you."

Instantly Tamara was on her feet upon the floor. And there, before her on the tiny table, was a large bouquet of roses.

"Oh, Brent," she whispered, "where did you get the flowers?"

"Mrs. Trimble down on Bully Creek grows them. She told me that if they were still blooming, she'd have some here. She also said that it would help you feel at home and that no bride should be without flowers. Do you like them?"

"Oh, I do. They're lovely!"

Tamara looked at her husband then, and saw the love-stricken look she had seen before, a look of such absolute devotion and longing that once again she panicked.

"And Brent," she said quickly as she turned away, "your home is so . . . so . . ."

A great clap of thunder literally shook the cabin, and Brent Beecher, pulled out of his reverie, spun toward the door. "Oh, my goodness," he yelped, "I forgot the team and the things in the wagon, and here comes the storm!"

Nor was Brent wrong. Even as he ran the horses and wagon toward the safety of the barn, large drops of rain splattered into the dusty soil. Seconds later the rain increased, and then lightning slammed into the hill above the barn. Instantly the thunder crashed down upon the tiny home, like a monster roaring of impending destruction. And then it seemed to the new Mrs. Beecher that the curtains of heaven were torn aside and all the windows thrown open at once.

Never had she seen such a torrential downpour. Sheets of violent rain streaked almost horizontally across the small valley, whipped along by the raging winds above. Numbly she stood watching, hoping that it would continue, hoping —well, to be honest, hoping that it would keep her new husband from coming back from the barn.

And so there it was. The admission. She really didn't want him to come back; she was too afraid to want that at all. In fact, she really didn't want to be married. Even just the thought of a man touching her, of being, well, *intimate* was the word her mother had used, filled her heart with stark terror.

Tamara didn't know why she felt that way. In fact, she supposed that it was a common feeling among women, though how so many of them overcame it eluded her completely. But it was a woman's problem, of that she was certain. Men simply didn't feel the things she was feeling. There was no such thing as a modest man—her younger brothers had shown her that over and over again. But a woman? And especially herself?

Oh, why hadn't she realized it earlier? She simply wasn't ready for marriage, and if she had used a little sense, she would have avoided it. But there had been so much pressure —from friends, family, and especially from Brent, who had courted her with all his heart and soul.

But maybe it wasn't too late. Maybe she could end this thing before it even started. If she could just talk to him, tell him that she wasn't ready yet, he would surely understand.

Or would he? No, Tamara admitted to herself, he wouldn't. Brent was understanding in all things, and he was as kind and gentle as anyone she had ever known. But he had wanted her for his wife and had haunted her every waking moment, as well as many of her sleeping ones, until he had convinced her that she also wanted him to be her husband. Now that their wedding had been accomplished, he would most certainly *not* be understanding about her desire to bring it to a hasty conclusion.

However, she didn't actually even have to talk to him, at least not directly. In fact, it would be a simple matter to go back to Vale or Ontario, telegraph her parents, and tell them that the whole idea had been a mistake, a tragic, terrible mistake. She need only take one of the horses when Brent wasn't watching, ride off, and be gone. He would find her gone, of course, and would want to come after her. But she would leave him a brief note of truthful explanation, and once he understood completely, he would be as relieved as she would be.

"Well," she said aloud as she searched for a pencil and paper, "what exactly are you going to tell him, Miss Tamara?"

That was a good question. So good, in fact, that even after she had the pencil and paper in hand, Tamara could not think of how to explain her fears to her new husband. Each idea she had sounded so foolish on paper that she crossed it out to begin again. When the page was finally filled with scratched-out half-thoughts, she finally gave it up.

"There," she said as she crumbled the paper and threw it in the cold, open fireplace. "I'll just go, and, later, if we ever meet again, well, I will explain things then."

Reaching behind the door, Tamara took up her cloak and wrapped it about herself, wondering whether she could get around to the rear of the barn for a horse and avoid Brent in the process. Hurriedly she crossed to the door, opened it, and was struck full in the face by the driving rain.

Taking a deep, determined breath, the frightened Tamara stepped out onto the porch, pulled the door shut behind her, and turned to face the not-so-distant barn. In that instant, she felt the hair on the back of her neck prickle and lift up, and she hesitated. There was a strange odor in the air. She started to turn to see what might be causing it, and in that fraction of a second, another bolt of lightning flashed, sizzling for what seemed forever atop the lightning rod which graced the barn roof, directly before her view.

Then the lightning was gone, and the whole world seemed to explode with crashing, crushing thunder. With a scream of renewed fear, the new Mrs. Brent Beecher fled back through the door, hastily pulled the cloak from her shoulders, and then stood in the middle of the room, hugging herself and trembling violently.

Well, one thing was sure. She wasn't going out in that storm! Not on her life was she stepping one foot outside that cabin door.

Instead, she was going to . . . she was . . .

And finally her tears came, matching the storm outside in intensity if not in volume, and Tamara Beecher fell to the floor of the cabin where she huddled alone, sobbing.

Later, when the rumble of thunder had finally subsided, Tamara rose to her feet, telling herself that after the storm there would still be time to leave. *Yes,* she thought as she rearranged her hair before the small, dim mirror, *when the storm lets up, then I can tell Brent how I feel and be on my way home. But until then . . .*

Oh, why had she married him? Why had she let Brent persuade her that she was ready? Why, oh why, had she gone through with it?

But wait! her mind suddenly shouted. That was an easy question. She loved him! From the very day she had met Brent she had loved him, loved everything about him. Besides being understanding, he was kind, gentle, firm when needed, intelligent, and even a little silly.

Why, in Boise, he had joined up with a group of young men who met every Saturday morning to play a game that some fellow named James Naismith had invented, back in 1892. It was a strange game called basketball, where each of the players tried to throw a ball through a bottomless peach basket that was nailed high on a wall.

Because of his height, Brent was good at the game and scored many points. But what amazed Tamara was that he could find so much enjoyment in such a silly game. He was so like a little boy that she could hardly believe it, so like her little brothers that it dumbfounded her. Yet that was one of the reasons she loved him so much, one of the reasons that she had agreed to marry him in the first place.

In fact, right now, through the window, shrouded by rain but still visible, she could see a fruit basket nailed to the side of his barn.

My goodness, she thought, *even here on his ranch—*

With a roar, the door burst open and a bedraggled, soaked-to-the-skin Brent Beecher skidded to a stop on the braided rug. Then he threw the door closed behind him and placed Tamara's two dripping suitcases upon the floor.

"Whew," he muttered as he wiped his dripping face on an equally wet sleeve, "wetter out there than the bottom of old Mrs. Malley's washtub."

"Y . . . yes," his bride agreed, "it looks like it."

"Did you see that lightning?" Brent asked as he pointed out of the window toward the barn. "The way my hair lifted, it must have been close!"

"It was," Tamara said, backing up a little. "It hit the lightning rod atop the barn."

"Truly? No wonder the horses acted so skittish. And the way my hair prickled, I thought sure I was a goner. I'm glad I put that rod up there last spring. I—Why, Tamara, you're all wet!"

Tamara looked down at herself in confusion. "I . . . uh . . . I went outside."

"You were worried about me, weren't you," Brent stated, his eyes showing his sudden comprehension. It was an assumption rather than a question, and the absolute awe in his voice both terrified and thrilled the new bride.

"Lawsy," Brent whispered as he stood, staring. "Never in my life, not since Ma died when I was a kid, have I had anybody to care about me, to worry over me. And now I do. Oh, lawsy, lawsy. . . . Heavenly Father, how can I ever thank thee for this wondrous little girl that thou hast brought into my lonely life?"

That was enough for Tamara, who was already so overwhelmed that she could hardly handle things. "I . . . uh . . . ," she sputtered, interrupting her new husband's spontaneous prayer, "you . . . you're sopped to the skin, Mr. Beecher. Better get out of those clothes before you catch your death of cold."

Brent finally looked down at his own bedraggled self, and at the puddle that was rapidly forming on the rough-hewn wood floor beneath him.

"Yeah," he said, shaking himself as if he were waking from a deep sleep. "Reckon I had." And without further ado, not even noticing that his wife was standing there watching him, Brent unbuttoned his collar and peeled it off. But then, as he reached up and unbuttoned the top buttons of his shirt, his eyes caught those of his new wife—and instantly froze.

"I . . . I . . . ," he stammered, suddenly unable to speak.

"What is it?" Tamara asked, so caught up in her own fears that she was absolutely unaware of what was troubling her new husband.

Brent, his soaking collar clutched in his trembling hand and his soaking shirt partly unbuttoned, was suddenly a bright red with embarrassment.

"I . . . ," he tried to explain, "I . . . uh . . . well . . . uh . . . You're watching, Tamara, and I . . . uh . . . Well, lawsy, girl, I just ain't used to . . . to . . . female critters watching me disrobe!"

And the new Mrs. Tamara Beecher, with eye-opening realization, finally understood that her husband was just as thoroughly frightened and confused by this marriage experience as was she.

Exulting with that secret knowledge and the surprising power of confidence that it gave her, she turned quickly away.

"You go ahead and change," she stated matter of factly but with relief-filled joy consuming her heart. "I'll get up a fire and maybe throw together a bite of something to eat. Then maybe if this storm keeps up, we may need to . . . to cuddle a little to stay warm."

And a long time later, when only the coals from the fire cast a dim red glow across the snug and lovely room, and when the only sounds in that room were the rain beating a heavy march upon the roof and the thunder drumming like horses' hooves upon the hills, Brent Beecher's new wife, Tamara, lay beside her sleeping husband on the comfortable feather tick of the old handmade bed, gazing up into the darkness.

She was dreaming; she was planning; but most of all, and thankfully, too, she was smiling.

"Thank you, Father in Heaven, for this wonderful storm," she whispered happily in a short, heartfelt prayer. "And thank you forever, dear Lord, for sending that lightning to keep me here where I belong."

Meanwhile, the storm, unconcerned with barns and log cabins below, continued to sweep south and east, building and growing—

DAY SIX

Tuesday, November 1, 1910

Raft River Mountains

Normally a weather front travels at a consistent speed of about 25 miles per hour, 24 hours per day. At this rate, 480 miles per day, any given storm may cross the entire continental United States in a little less than a week. However, if the jet stream has created a series of migrating shortwave troughs, these troughs will carve out a position in the atmosphere called a longwave trough. These longwave troughs are very persistent, lasting from a week to two weeks. Cold fronts occasionally stall in these longwave troughs, building up more energy as they churn in place. This not only has the effect of lengthening the storm's travel time but also makes the storm's effects more severe.

By November 1, 1910, the polar jet stream is leveling out in its deep southward curve, and our cold front, caught in a longwave trough such as we have described, begins a very slow sweep that will bring it further eastward. The front is also climbing again as the land rises to the south of the Snake River Plain, slowly cooling the huge air mass. At this point a portion of the front hits the Raft River Mountains, a low range of hills that straddles the connecting borders of Utah, Idaho, and Nevada. As the front is forced up over these hills, it brings about an even more rapid rise in elevation, and a similarly rapid cooling. The end result is snow.

Snowflakes form when water vapor changes directly to ice, rather than first to water droplets and then to ice. In scientific jargon, this is called sublimation, *and it will happen in a cloud only when the temperature in that cloud is below freezing. The temperature on the ground ahead of such a storm makes little difference and can be as high as eighty degrees only hours before a snowstorm. The temperature in the clouds and behind the front determine the nature of the precipitation, not what is before the front.*

As a final note on snow, the vast variety of intricate and beautiful patterns of snowflakes are infinite in number but are always hexagonal. As such hexagonal-shaped ice crystals begin to fall in the Raft River Mountains, two brothers out alone in the storm lift their coat collars apprehensively.

TREASURE

Craig Connely sat on the back of his mule, gazing thoughtfully up at the clouded, churning sky. Up the slope behind him, his brother Bart did the same.

"What do you think?" Bart called down, his voice almost lost in the howling wind.

For a moment Craig didn't answer. Instead he considered, doing as he had done all of his life, holding back speech until he had done his best to assay all the facts. Around them, the wind was shrieking fiercely, and the sentinel pines on the ridge above Goose Creek were whipping as though giants' hands were shaking them, brushing them down. He had never seen the wind blow so hard, and that troubled him deeply.

He also worried because the temperature had dropped so far so quickly. Whereas hours earlier he had been too warm to wear a coat, now his ears, especially the one that had been frostbitten back in 1905, were stinging badly in the cold. Then, too, the pack animals were skittish, all three of them, as were the mounts he and his brother were riding. Five skittish mules and two nervous men had to mean something, he decided.

"I think," he shouted to Bart, "that this is a storm we are looking into, and a bad one. Even though it's still morning, I expect we'd better find us a hole."

"I'm with you," Bart called back.

"Miserable, ornery, no-good, lousy, good-for-nothing storm!" Craig then cussed as he searched the hills with his eyes. "Confound it for not waiting until next week when we would have been home with our families!"

"Craig," Bart asked when his older brother had finished cursing the storm, "you been in this part of these hills before?"

"Once, but that was years back, when I was real small. This area was where Dad herded sheep one summer, and I spent a few days with him."

"If he was here, and you knew it, then why haven't we ever looked here before?"

"Well, like I said, Bart, he was only here that one summer. On the other hand, he spent eight or nine summers over on the Jarbridge drainage, so that's where I've always figured it had to be. But since we haven't found anything over there, I thought maybe it wouldn't hurt to at least spend a day or so in this area before we head back."

"So, what are these hills called?"

"I'm pretty sure they're called the Goose Creeks. That's what Dad called them, anyway. But the whole range is called the Raft Rivers. They lie on the corner of where Utah and Nevada butt up against Idaho, and Goose Creek flows some in all three states, as well. However, I'm just not exactly certain where, in the midst of all that gorgeous but unprofitable geography, we're located right now."

"Unprofitable is right!" Bart growled as he spurred his mule down beside Craig's. "What is this, the thirtieth day?"

"Either that or the thirty-first."

"Well, it doesn't matter. It's a month, no matter how you cut it—another month out of our lives, wasted. I'm just glad we're on our way home."

"You sure it's wasted?" Craig asked curtly.

"I hope to shout! I've done everything I know how to do in the past month, and so have you, yet we've found nothing that even looks promising. If Dad really found gold over on the Jarbridge, you can bet that *we'll* never find it."

"Maybe next year we'll do better."

"Next year? Craig, you can't be serious. I'm not about to waste the rest of my life on the back of a stubborn mule on a fool's errand after gold."

Craig smiled. "Well, Dad always said that gold was a hard-found thing."

"That he most certainly did. According to you, he also said there were mountains of it out in this country. What I've never understood is, if there are mountains of gold out here, why didn't he ever bring any of it home with him?"

"How do you know he didn't?" Craig asked quietly.

"What?"

Craig Connely smiled. "Bart, I don't have time for wild goose chases, either. I'd never have come out here if I hadn't seen something that convinced me that Dad was telling the truth."

"You serious?"

"Dead."

"Likely," Bart said disgustedly, and then immediately changed the subject to show his scorn for his brother's comment. "But so will we be dead, happen we don't find us that hole you mentioned."

"Then leave us be looking for the same, Mr. Connely."

"After you, Mr. Connely," Bart grinned thinly. And together the two brothers started down the steep and rocky slope.

For thirty minutes they rode in silence, the only sounds being the wind, the creaking of saddles, and the occasional clicks of mule hooves against stone. Both men were thinking of home and families, and both were wishing that the storm had held off for another two or three days. Given that much more time, they would have been out of the hills. Then the winter could have raged all it wished, and they wouldn't have minded. It was frustrating, though, to know they were so near to being finished, and then to have to hole up and sit out a storm with nothing more profitable to do than wait.

No doubt they thought too of their past thirty days of wasted effort. In all their climbing and digging and searching on the Jarbridge, Bruneau, Sheep Creek, and East Fork drainages in southern Idaho and northern Nevada and Utah, they had found absolutely nothing that looked even remotely promising.

Oh, there'd been a little color, placer gold, scattered here and there in the streams, but not enough to make panning it worthwhile. And neither of them had been able to follow the color up.

Placer gold is merely gold that has washed out of some ledge or outcropping of goldbearing rock, usually quartz. The gold is washed downslope during storms and spring melts, ending in streams where it is again washed along until its weight forces it into the mud and silt of the stream bottom. There it gradually sinks to bedrock.

If it has been washed a considerable distance, the nuggets will be rounded and smooth. If not, they will be more rough. By this gauge, a man may know about how far he is from his gold source, that place he fondly calls his mother lode.

But for Craig and Bart Connely, their search for such a mother lode had been fruitless and hopelessly frustrating. Oh, they had found one small pocket of gold on a gravel bank near the steep slopes of Copper Mountain where Jarbridge Creek headed. But the nuggets, all very small, had been well rounded. Upstream, where there should have been more, they had found nothing, not for miles and miles. Geologically it made no sense, but it was still frustratingly true.

Yet the two brothers had kept on, using their limited knowledge of geology to try to locate an outcropping of goldbearing rock, or even a place where things looked likely enough to warrant running a stope into the hill.

They had also looked constantly for landmarks—clumps of trees, rock formations, or even uniquely designed canyons—that their father had described to Craig in the last years of his life. Some of these they had found, places where the old sheepherder had left his lonely mark upon the land, or spots which he found to be of such unsurpassed beauty that he could never stop describing them. On trees near where he had camped they had found carved his brand, the Flying C, or occasionally his initials, sometimes with the date of his camp. On the face of a cliff in another area they had once again found his initials and the date, and read with interest that a bear he had killed that day was lying directly below. Of course the brothers could not locate any of the bones, it had been so many years since the kill.

The lonely sheepherder had also erected occasional rock piles for one reason or another, and invariably the brothers would find, in the center of such piles, a stone with their father's name and the date scratched on it. However, even with such markers, the two men could never understand what their father had been trying to mark or call attention to.

And so with all their searching, and with all their success in piecing together these elements of the lonely years of their father's life, not once had they found anything that might direct them toward the lost gold mine that had played such a prominent part in recent family legend.

Now their annual fall prospecting season was past, and they had nothing but a few nuggets and a small poke of gold dust to show for their efforts. It was discouraging, to say the least. But like Craig was saying, maybe next year.

"Bart, the snow's here."

Bart pulled his sheepskin coat more tightly about his neck. "Yeah," he growled. "I noticed. How much food you reckon we have left?"

"Well, if we go easy on it, there's maybe a week's worth. I'm more worried about feed for the mules."

"Do you think it'll get that deep?"

Craig nodded. "It could, the way it's already coming down. And this wind could cause some terrible drifting. I say we'd better find our hole down in the bottoms, where we can get at the cottonwoods and alders and willows. Comes to it, the mules can live on that stuff and make it."

"Sounds good to me. You know, I've been minding a dent in the hill off to our left there. You see it?"

"You mean below that low-hanging cliff?"

"That's the one."

"Interesting," Craig responded. "I've been noticing the same dimple."

"Well, it doesn't look like much from here, but then neither does anywhere else in these miserable, barren hills. But I do see some trees there, so it might work out all right for the mules."

"Sounds good, little brother," Craig declared with a wide grin. "Let us be checking it out."

The dimple, when the Connely brothers got to it, proved to be a narrow defile of a canyon. It could not have been more than two or three hundred yards from where it began on the face of the mountain, right below the small cliff, to where it mouthed out above a tiny spring and stream. Near the mouth, however, the canyon floor leveled out for about thirty feet, and the floor of the defile was almost that wide. The sides of the canyon rose steeply for perhaps forty feet and then leveled off into the sides of the mountain.

In short, it seemed the perfect spot to weather out a wild Norther like the one sweeping in upon them.

"Plenty of deadfalls here," Craig stated as they halted their mules on the grassy bottom. "Won't lack for firewood."

"Or forage," Bart added. "Grass is almighty thick, and there's plenty of sweet cottonwood bark, if we need it. I'll set up the tent against that old cottonwood blow down and get a fire going."

"Good. I'll rub down the mules and see if I can block off the mouth of this draw so they won't drift. If I can do that, we shouldn't have too much to worry about."

Both brothers went quickly to work, and within another thirty minutes they had made camp and were preparing a hot meal of frybread and beans.

"This is a great camping spot," muttered Bart as he leaned back under the large old deadfall a little later. "In fact, I'll bet it'd be good enough for Governor Brady himself, happen he was crazy enough to be out here in a storm like this."

"I'll say. Him and ex-Governor Gooding, too. This place has been used as a camp before this, and you're right, it's a good one. We're getting a little snow down here, but that wind can blow all she wants, and we won't feel much of it. All it'll do is drift a little snow over the sides."

"Folks have camped here before, you say?"

"Probably not recently," Craig declared. "There are cut poles at the mouth, though, so I'd say someone fenced this off some time in the past. I used 'em, and most of 'em still worked just fine, though a couple were starting to rot. Then when I was gathering wood, I saw some stacked poles back where the draw narrows down and starts climbing. They were all rotten, though, so it's been quite a spell since they were cut."

"Who do you think they were?"

"The folks who used this hide-out? Who knows? Mountainmen like Peter Ogden, Finan McDonald, and Thomas Fitzpatrick were all through this country. Could have been them, though I don't know what they might have wanted poles for.

"Then, too, it might have been some wandering miner. After the California gold rush died out, men drifted in from everywhere—looking, looking, looking. Those poles are thick, and they might have been cut as timbers for a shaft some old miner was digging somewhere."

"Miner, huh?" Bart mused. "You know, there's a small hill right back here against the hillside. I saw it when I was gathering firewood. I never gave it a thought, but now that I do, it looks mighty like the tailings from somebody's digging."

"Are you serious?" Craig questioned, leaning back against the dead tree. "Now, that's mighty interesting, it surely is."

"Why?"

"I told you a little while ago that I wouldn't be on this chase unless I had something more than Dad's years-old stories. But you didn't seem to want to hear what I had to say."

Bart smiled. "I didn't mean to be rude, Craig, but I'm filled way up to here with stories of Dad's lost gold mines."

"So you don't want to hear this?"

"Have I heard it before?"

Now Craig smiled. "Nope."

"Why not?"

Slowly Craig reached out and poked at the fire. "No reason, really. It's just that, well, this was always sort of a special memory to me. And besides, I didn't want to get your hopes up too high."

Bart laughed. "Well, big brother, you don't need to worry about that one anymore."

"So you want to hear it?"

"Why not? So far as I can see, there isn't much of an alternative, at least as far as entertainment is concerned. Have at your tale, Craig, and I'll listen."

"All right, Bart, here she is. I recollect seeing some actual gold the night Dad got back from his last jaunt with the sheep."

"You mean when he came home hurt?"

"That's right."

"I can't believe you never told me this before."

Craig stared into the flames. "I know. I've been about to tell you more than once, but one thing or another interrupted me, and so I saved it, waiting for a better time."

"And this is it?"

"I reckon so," Craig replied with a wide smile.

"And?" Bart growled. "What else do you remember that you haven't ever told me?"

"Bart," Craig responded, leaning forward, "listen to me. Dad showed Mother and me a rock as big as his fist. I'll never forget how it glinted golden in the lamplight. I remember he and Mother laughed a little as they looked at it, and I also remember that he told her to get rid of it."

"You serious?"

"I am."

"But . . . why?"

Craig grinned. "You know what Dad was like. Everything in his life had to be hard. Otherwise he didn't feel like he was living the gospel and earning his blessings."

"But he was dying! You'd think he would have wanted to take care of Mother and all us kids."

"That's what he thought he was doing, Bart. I don't know what he expected Mother to do for a living, but I distinctly remember him telling her that he didn't want any of us wasting our lives chasing off on a fool's errand after gold. That's why he wanted her to get rid of that rock."

"Did she?"

"I hope to shout she did! Have you ever seen it?"

Slowly Bart shook his head.

"Neither have I, not since that night. Just before she died, I asked Mother what she had done with it. You see, I always sort of thought she had hidden it. Either that or cashed it in. But not her. No sir, Mother had done just as Dad had told her to do. She had gotten rid of it—literally thrown it out. It's probably still lying there, too, right where she threw it. I just don't happen to know where that particular location was."

"Dad really didn't want us hunting gold like this, did he?"

Craig looked at his younger brother. "No, he didn't. But then, that was being a little hypocritical, too, which is why I haven't paid any attention to his wishes. You see, Bart, his whole life through Dad never stopped looking for gold. He was always after that one big strike. Crazy thing is, I think he found it."

"Yeah," Bart declared as he shifted position before the fire, "but according to Mother, his looking was a mistake that he always regretted."

"What are you talking about?"

"I'm talking about Dad's life," Bart replied. "According to Mother, Dad felt like he should have lived it differently."

Craig laughed. "That's nuts, Bart. He was a sheepherder, he prospected on the side, and he loved doing both with all his heart and soul."

Stubbornly Bart shook his head. "According to Mother, that wasn't altogether true. In fact, she told me once that Dad had been offered a position with the railroad, which he took. It was a wonderful job, and it offered them real security. He and Mother both knew that the Lord had blessed him with that job, but he only lasted with it through one winter. Then the lure of that unfound mother lode drew him back into the hills, and he spent the rest of his life herding sheep for a living, which he hated, so he could chase after his golden dream. That's how come I can't even remember him, and you can only remember a little. He was never around, Craig, and Mother told me that he died regretting it."

For a moment there was silence, and the popping of the wood in the fire was the only intrusion into the distant moaning of the wind.

"I guess that's why I want to find his gold so badly," Craig declared softly. "With that kind of money, a man could afford to spend every waking minute with his family. That's what I would like to do."

"What about your career?"

Craig laughed. "That's no career, Bart. It's a job, and I'd quit it in a minute if I found that gold. Yes sir, I would love to retire and take it easy with my family for the rest of my life."

"Do you think that would teach your kids proper values?"

"I don't think it would hurt. Say, what gives, little brother? Where do you get off giving me the third degree about hunting for gold? If I'm not mistaken, it's you sitting right across the fire from me, just as you have every other night for the past month. And we did the same thing together last year, and the year before that, too. And now you're acting all high and mighty about me finding gold and getting rich?"

"You're right," Bart replied slowly. "But I'll tell you this, Craig. I've been doing a lot of thinking about this quest you and I have set ourselves on, and the longer I look at it, the less I like it. In all our searching, we've never found enough gold to buy supper with, let alone get rich on. Yet we've spent, in time and effort and actual cash outlay, a good year's salary for one man, maybe two.

"Worse, we've deprived ourselves of three months' company with our wives and children, not to mention all the evenings you and I have spent hidden out in your back room, dreaming and planning while our families sat off alone.

"And let's talk about our kids. To my way of thinking, we've done about what Dad did with us, which both of us feel a little bitter about. I wonder if our kids will grow up feeling a little bitter about us?"

Craig leaned back and looked up at the swaying trees, but his thoughts were not on the wind and the storm, not at all. "It's only for one month a year," he finally argued.

"Right. Plus dozens and dozens of evenings. You know, the bishop even released me from the Sunday School super-intendency when he found out I was doing this again. I don't know if I feel good about that, and I know darn well that he didn't. He flat out told me so. And now you want to do it again next year. I don't know, Craig. I just don't know."

Reaching down, Craig tossed another length of wood on the fire. Then he looked at his younger brother. "I have one last question, Bart."

"What is it?"

"Suppose we did find Dad's gold. Can you sit there look-ing me in the eye and tell me honestly that you would walk away from it?"

"I would," Bart replied seriously.

"What? I don't believe you!"

"I didn't finish," Bart replied as a slow smile spread across his face. "I'd walk away, all right, but I'd do it with every pocket I had stuffed full of gold, and with the claim completely staked."

"Hah!" Craig laughed. "I knew it!"

"Of course you did. I may be worried, but that doesn't make me stupid. Now, I will say this, big brother. That ap-plies to this year only. I want you to get used to the idea that come next fall, you'll be doing this alone. I've even prayed about this, and I'm not leaving my family by choice again, not ever."

"You've prayed about it?" Craig asked incredulously.

Bart nodded.

"Interesting."

"How so?"

"Oh, it just is. I'm the oldest, and here I've never even thought of doing that—praying about the gold, that is."

"Maybe you ought to," Bart said easily.

Slowly Craig nodded. "Maybe so. But on the other hand, little brother, maybe I won't need to."

"Oh? And why not?"

"Because while you've been preaching," Craig replied with a wide and teasing grin, "I've been thinking, remember-ing. I haven't thought of this in a long time, maybe since that night when I was a kid. But it has just come to me, sitting here, that Dad—the night he showed Mother and me that rock of gold—told us that he had found it in a tiny canyon, almost like a wrinkle in the flat face of the mountain. He told her, too, that there was a cliff heading that wrinkle. He'd done some digging there, he told her, and had found the ore in the most unlikely looking spot he'd ever seen. Almost like a dirt bank, he said. At least that's my memory of his story."

"You were almighty young then."

"I was. I would have been seven."

"He never mentioned it again?"

"Not that I know of. Neither did Mother. I can't believe I've never thought of that little tidbit, though, until tonight."

"Hard to remember that many years."

"I know."

Silently Craig took up his stick and stirred the fire again, and the only sound was the distant howling of the wind and a little sizzling as occasional snowflakes drifted into the heat of the fire.

"Well," Bart finally drawled, "there's a cliff up there that heads this draw."

"I know."

"This canyon might be called a wrinkle."

"I know that, too."

"That little hill I found? The slope behind it looks to be mostly a gray sort of clay. Mighty unpromising-looking dirt bank."

"Interesting."

"Isn't it."

Above the brothers, the wind howled across the face of the mountain, driving the snow before it. A log in the fire popped, sending a small shower of sparks flying upward, and below them one of the mules brayed plaintively. Beyond that there was silence, and in it the brothers sat together, thinking.

"Uh . . . Bart," Craig finally spoke, "you want to show me where those tailings are?"

Bart grinned. "Only if your schedule's not too busy, big brother. Wouldn't want to bother you none, the storm coming on us like it is."

Craig smiled back. Casually then, and yet with a stirring of anxiety, the two brothers climbed to their feet, took up their shovels, and made their way through the skiff of snow to the small hill in question, which lay not more than a half-dozen yards from their fire.

The slope behind the hill was nondescript and at first glance held nothing. But Craig, poking around, suddenly felt his shovel slide through the earth beneath a small brush. There it hit only space, and no matter how deeply he pushed the shovel, that was all he felt.

"You see that?" he asked as his heart began to pound.

"I see it."

"You up to a little backbreaking work?"

"If you are."

While the snow swirled and fell around him, Craig took a deep breath to steady his nerves, and then he began carefully to throw dirt down the hill behind him. Bart stood at his side digging just as quickly, and before long a hole opened up that was obviously the entrance to a small shaft of fairly early origin.

With excitement swelling within them, the two brothers bore down on the hill. Their pace quickened, and before long was at a fever pitch, which continued without letting up until ultimately they found themselves standing in the shelter of the old mine shaft, looking around.

The shaft they had uncovered was not more than nine or ten feet deep and was only high enough to permit a standing man for the first four or five feet. Yet a lot of work had been done there, and the brothers could see that whoever had dug it had spent quite a bit of time and energy doing so.

"Craig," Bart said quietly as he lit a candle and held it high, "are you seeing what I'm seeing?"

"I . . . reckon," Craig stammered as he lit and held out his own candle.

There, in a downward slope across the rear face of the old mine shaft, was an eighteen-inch-wide seam of rock and metal that sparkled bright gold in the flickering light of the brothers' candles.

"Do . . . do you think it's real?"

"Real enough," Craig breathed. "Do you think these are Dad's diggings?"

"If they aren't," Bart responded, his voice still hushed, "he'd have wished they were. He'd have wanted badly to see this."

"He did see it," Craig suddenly said as he held his candle closer to the wall. "Looky here."

Bart leaned closer, and there on the wall were his father's initials and the date, written apparently with the burnt end of a stick.

"Isn't that date just before he died?"

Craig nodded. "It is. I was seven the year he wrote this."

"Do you suppose this is where he got his rock that you saw?"

Again Craig nodded. "It had to be. I'll bet he got hurt right here in this draw, or else shortly after he left."

"Amazing. And to think I wasn't sure if I believed your story about that golden rock."

"You'll learn, little brother," Craig responded with a smile. "Look. Here's something else he wrote. Can you make it out?"

Leaning closer, Bart tried, but finally gave it up. "Not without my specs, big brother. You'll have to do it for both of us."

Nodding, Craig leaned in and, with the candle held close, began to read.

"I've spent all my life hunting this lode," the charcoal-penned message read, "and now that I have finally found it, the Lord has shown me what an utter fool I have turned out to be. I'm heading home."

Straightening, Craig gave a long look at his silent younger brother. "Sounds like he meant what he told Mother about us hunting gold," he finally said.

"Sounds like it."

"Looks like your prayers were right on target, too."

"Looks that way, all right."

"I'll tell you something else, too," Craig said slowly.

"What's that?" Bart asked.

"That's the last time I'll ever cuss a storm. Even a Nor'wester. Finding this mine of Dad's sure makes it all seem worthwhile."

Bart laughed, and then, while the ferocious storm raged across the mountains around them, the two brothers turned their backs to the old mine shaft and quietly and soberly walked away from their own personal mountain of brilliantly glittering, but mostly worthless, iron pyrites—*fool's gold.*

Wednesday, November 2, 1910

Ogden Canyon

As the storm clouds along the edge of our cold front drop out of the Raft River Mountains and sweep across northern Utah and the Great Salt Lake, the slight and very uneven warming of the air mass brings a combination of rain, sleet, and snow.

Sleet—or frozen raindrops—forms when raindrops from the upper air fall through a layer of air where the temperature is below freezing. These frozen drops then reach the earth in the form of small bits of ice. In the same cloud, in the area that is below freezing, snow is also forming and falling earthward. And only a few hundred feet away a mass of air has warmed to above freezing, thus giving birth to rain.

Churning across the state, this rather convoluted front slams directly into the Wasatch Mountains, and a scenario unfolds identical to that played out when the front hit the Cascade and Raft River mountains. The prevailing westerly winds push the front up and over the steep slopes, the air cools dramatically as it rises, and though moisture falls prodigiously, once again it is in the form of snow.

This is not particularly good news for a young couple who have decided to spend the night camping in Ogden Canyon.

A KINGDOM OR AN EMPIRE

"You're awfully quiet."

Dwayne Jenkins looked to his right, where his wife, Hilary, was seated in the passenger seat of their new Pierce Arrow touring car. She did not respond but instead lifted the collar of her duster against the wind, which had shifted in the past few minutes from the south to the north and was suddenly blowing very cold.

"Hilary, what's the matter?"

Still the young woman did not look at him. But after she had adjusted the bow under her chin which held her hat in place, she did condescend to speak—slowly.

"I'm sorry, Dwayne," she said, the catch in her voice evident. "I . . . I just saw something in you this week that . . . that I hadn't suspected was there. Now I . . . I don't know exactly how to feel."

"Are you still upset about me buying this automobile?"

"It's more than that, and you know it!"

And Dwayne did know it, too. This time he had truly offended his wife. The trouble was, he wasn't at all certain that he cared. But that wasn't quite right, either. In fact, he did care. Just maybe not enough to do anything about it.

So how had this latest bump in their year-old marriage come about? Innocently enough, of course, as had all the previous bumps they had managed to get across. He and Hilary had made the trip by train from Denver to Salt Lake City so that they could have their marriage solemnized in the Salt Lake Temple. That was all well and good, and it had been what both of them had wanted. But then he had found that floating poker game operating down the hall from their room in the hotel, and the damage had been done.

Dwayne, a first-year practicing attorney, was working for a large firm in Denver. But his pay was not yet what he had hoped to be making, and since he had learned a little about card playing as a youngster, and since the trip to Salt Lake City had been quite expensive, the game had been too enticing.

The trouble, therefore, was twofold. First, Hilary was utterly and absolutely opposed to gambling. Second, he had promised her that during their week in Salt Lake City, he and she would attend as many endowment sessions in the temple as they could, doing work on her diligently researched family line. However, the game, which had run for three days and two nights, had thoroughly kaboshed their plan. He had been to one session in the temple, the one preceding their own sealing ceremony, but because of the game he had not had time to go back again.

Of course, his poker had been fantastic! He had played skillfully and had won well over five thousand dollars, a tremendous boon to their struggling economic situation. But even though they now owned a totally paid for new automobile, which would be shipped home on the same train in which they traveled, and which would wow everyone in Denver, and even though they still had a great deal of cash left over to take home with them, Hilary was still not happy.

And she had let him know it, too. Torn between love for him, she had said, and an inspired revulsion of the worldliness in which he had become entrapped, which she did not find appealing at all, Hilary had gone to the temple alone. There, she later explained to Dwayne, she had spent two or three prayerful hours, thoughtfully pleading for divine direction. In her prayer she had explained to the Lord that her husband was not a bad man. Rather, she felt that he was a very good man who had become caught up in what seemed to her to be a bad thing. She had then pleaded with the Lord to please provide for her a way to explain those feelings to Dwayne.

Later, in the privacy of their hotel room, she had finally broached the subject of her discomfort with him.

"Hey," Dwayne had responded teasingly, "I made nearly five thousand bucks, honey. They tell me I'm the biggest winner of the year. I'm really on a roll."

"Is that so important, Dwayne?" she had questioned. "That you get more money? Is that all you ever dream about?"

Dwayne had turned to look at his bride. "What is this, Hil? Are you trying to out-lawyer me?"

"I just want to know."

"Why?"

Hilary had sighed. "Honey, since you won't answer my questions, I'll answer yours. I want to know because I saw a side of you the past few days that I had not seen before, or at least not noticed. I saw a side that enjoyed gambling and willingly participated in it. I saw a side that would rather spend time doing Satan's work than the Lord's. I saw a side that was willing to do all of that just to accumulate money."

"You make me sound pretty dark," Dwayne had responded, fighting back his defensive urge to anger.

"I don't mean to," Hilary had replied softly. "I just want to better understand the man I chose to accompany me as my life's companion—and to help me inherit the celestial kingdom."

Well, Dwayne thought as he guided the new automobile up the winding mountain road with his silent wife beside him, fortunately he had been in a position where he could quit the game. They had then gone to one last session together in the temple and then had driven to Ogden to begin the journey by rail back to Denver.

But a storm in the Sierras had delayed the train, and so he had suggested that he and Hilary spend one night camping in the canyon, near a cave he had once discovered when he had been camping there as a boy. Hilary had agreed, they had quickly purchased some camping gear, and now here they were heading into the mountains east of Ogden, Utah.

"That wind has certainly turned cold," Hilary suddenly said as she again adjusted the collar of her new duster.

"True enough," Dwayne agreed. "But it has been real warm the past few days, so I don't think we need to worry about a storm. I think the wind is colder because we're higher up is all."

"Brrrrr. I hope so! How much further do we have to go?"

"Not much. I'm glad this road is here. They told me down at the depot that I could drive all the way."

"And where are we?"

Dwayne smiled. "Well, we came up Ogden Canyon, but right now we're in what's called Johnson Draw. Up ahead a little way is a campground where we'll stay."

"Will there be other people there?"

"Say, how would I know that? And why do you ask?"

Hilary shrugged. "Oh, I just get nervous if I'm camping around a lot of other people. Are . . . are you sure this is a road?"

Dwayne grunted as the car bounced over a large rock. "Well, it was supposed to be a road. I hope we don't have another flat tire. That one back there at the junction was hard to change."

"Don't we have a repair kit?"

"We are supposed to have one. I paid for one, that is certain. Maybe after we stop I will be able to find it. I hope . . . say, this looks like the place we're looking for."

"This is a campground?" Hilary asked with a giggle as they arrived at their destination. "Dwayne, are you serious? This is beautiful, for heaven's sake! I thought all public campgrounds were ugly with trash."

Dwayne grinned widely. "I told you that you would like it."

"I love it!" Hilary laughed, and in spite of Dwayne's frustration over his wife's narrow-minded approach to life, he marveled at the sound of her laughter—a tinkling of tiny bells in a palace of crystal. She was such a delight, this girl, this woman he had chosen to be his wife. Never in his wildest dreams had he ever imagined that he would be so fortunate as to be married to a person like her. If only she wouldn't worry so much about how he looked at money.

"I'll tell you the truth, Dwayne," Hilary said as she sat in the silent automobile, looking around. "This place is beautiful, but the wind really feels like the beginning of a storm."

"Come on, Hil, relax. We'll only be here until tomorrow, so even if it does storm a little, it won't be that bad. Even a city girl like you can enjoy roughing it in the wilderness once in a while."

Hilary laughed again. "Roughing it? In a public campground? My dear, you have a strange way of roughing it."

"Well, it was roughing it when I was here as a boy. But this campground isn't the end of it, either. Tomorrow we'll climb to the cave I told you about, the one I found when I was twelve. Then we'll see how you handle roughing it in the real wilderness."

"I'll handle it, dear worldly husband of mine," Hilary replied with a wink. "But even if it turns out that I actually enjoy this campout nonsense, I'm not going to let up on you. You deserve a little persecution. I try for a week to get you out of that poker game, and when you finally leave, you take me out in a storm to a public campground in some tiny little canyon filled with dirt and bugs—"

Throwing his arm around his new wife, Dwayne dragged her toward him across the seat of his new Pierce Arrow. "Persecution," he quipped as he began tickling her in the ribs, "we'll see who persecutes whom!"

"Dwayne!"

"It won't do you any good to plead for mercy. This time you've gone too far."

"Maybe," Hilary gasped, "and maybe not. But if you don't start steering your beloved automobile, it soon will have."

The coasting vehicle was straightened and once again brought to a halt, and shortly a camp was set up in the deserted campground. Then Dwayne set about preparing supper.

"Grief, Hil," he said with wonder as he worked, "this place has hardly changed at all. My memory is that there was a spring somewhere along there, because I remember playing in those rocks up above it. There wasn't anything like a pond or anything, because it was more of a seep than a big spring. But you could certainly get enough water to drink and have great water fights, and this grassy place is exactly where we pitched our tents.

"I'll bet you that if we climbed up there and looked, the spring would be there just like it was—"

"Dwayne," Hilary interrupted excitedly, "look. Bunny rabbits. Baby bunny rabbits, one, two . . . no, four of them! There in the grass. Oh, Dwayne, aren't they darling?"

"They *are* kind of cute," Dwayne said easily. "Think our kids will be that cute?"

"You mean all fuzzy, like you?" Hilary teased.

"No," Dwayne shot back, also teasingly. "I mean long-eared, like you're becoming with those lobe-stretching earrings you wear."

This time Hilary attacked Dwayne's ribs, and for a moment they did nothing but tickle each other. Slowly, however, that dissolved into a tender embrace, and moments later, when their lips finally met, Hilary realized once again how much she loved this man who had become her husband.

A few moments later, shivering in the cold, gusty wind, Hilary drew a sweater close about her and sat on a rock before the fire. Then she watched in amazement as Dwayne deftly prepared some of the food they had brought with them. Only when it was cooking in the hot coals near the edge of the fire did Dwayne come and sit down beside his wife.

"You do that very well," Hilary said earnestly. "How did you learn to cook over an open fire?"

"On my mission," Dwayne replied quietly. "We were out in the country most of the time, and I ate a lot of meals just like this, in the darkness over a little campfire."

"Did you like your mission?"

"Yeah," Dwayne replied quietly. "My mission was great. I loved the people, and I loved teaching them the gospel. I hated the poverty, though. It scared me, and I vowed I would never raise a family under conditions like that."

Hilary looked over at her husband. "Is that why you waited so long to get married?"

"Exactly. I'm not making a mint yet, Hil, but for a first-year attorney, I'm not doing badly, either. You could have done worse. Before we're through, maybe I'll be another Andrew Carnegie, John Jacob Astor, or Cornelius Vanderbilt. Those people keep yachts, servants, dozens of autos, horses and stables—"

"That's right," Hilary interrupted quietly. "They keep everything but the Ten Commandments."

Dwayne looked at his wife. "I'm being serious, Hil."

"So am I, Dwayne. You and I just covenanted to put all our energies into building Christ's kingdom. But now, listening to you, I can't help but conclude that your only desire is to build your own personal empire."

"What's wrong with having money, Hil? A fellow that has money is just that much more able to build the kingdom."

"If he'll use it for that, and if he's still the least bit interested in the kingdom."

"Well, you don't need to worry about me, Hil. I will be. But like it or not, I have the touch, and if you give me a few years, you'll never want for anything else as long as you live."

For a moment Hilary gazed at her new husband, wondering, but then she took his arm and pulled him close. "I already have everything I want, dear. Except, that is, for five or six children."

Dwayne laughed. "I hope that is one wish you *don't* have fulfilled. I meant it a couple of weeks ago when I told you I didn't want more than two, maybe three kids. Any more than that, they get lost in the shuffle, just like I did. Hil, I want my kids to have everything I didn't have. Clothes, a room of their own, a decent allowance, a house in a neighborhood they can be proud of. Our apartment is fine for now, but I won't raise children in that neighborhood. In a year or so we'll get us a home in the proper sort of neighborhood, surrounded by decent, important people. By next year I'll be making double what I am now, Hil, and double that two years later. We'll do just fine, honey. I promise you that."

Hilary nodded. "I'm sure we will. But Dwayne, honey, wouldn't you like to have six children, or maybe seven? After all, if you'll be making so much money—"

"No way," Dwayne stated flatly. "Three's tops."

"Don't I have a say in this, too?"

Dwayne looked at his wife's lovely face, now lit more by the flickering fire than by the deepening twilight. "Sure you do," he replied easily. "We'll have as many little rug rats as you want. But we'll start out one at a time, and by the time you get to three, well, you'll see what I mean. You ready to eat?"

For a moment Hilary gazed deeply into her husband's eyes, once again wondering, once again praying. But then, quickly, she smiled. "Hmmmm. It smells wonderful!"

"Come and get it, then," Dwayne declared as he stood and stepped to the fire, "before I throw it out to the coyotes and the wolves."

And with a smile of his own, Dwayne handed his young wife her first outdoor supper, and they quietly ate together.

"Are there really coyotes and wolves out there?" Hilary asked suddenly.

It had been long dark, the air was much colder, and the dying fire was casting only occasional flickering bursts of light against the wall of the tent. In the darkness and the cold inside, Hilary was huddled against her husband, but her eyes were wide with concern and her ears were straining to sort out the strange night sounds that were coming from just beyond the fabric borders of her world.

"Probably," Dwayne replied with a teasing grin. "And bears and mountain lions, too."

"Dwayne!"

"Hey," he replied as he wrapped his arms more tightly around his wife, "I'll tell you anything if it will get you to snuggle closer."

"You . . . pest," she giggled as she pulled playfully away. "Where did you ever get this idea for camping out, anyway?"

"From my grandparents. They lived here in Utah, and they were so broke when they got married that they spent their entire honeymoon camping on a mountain down in Sanpete County. It was all they could afford."

"Did anything happen to them?"

"Yeah, I'll say. They got rained on, when they got home everything smelled like smoke, they got dirty, and the first or second night they were there, a bear came down out of the timber and spent a few minutes sniffing around their tent, trying to figure out how to get inside."

"Truly? What did they do?"

Dwayne smiled. "Do? Well, I guess they got real quiet, and Grandpa told me it was difficult for him to breathe, Grandma was squeezing him so hard. They did something else, too, but I can't seem to remember . . .

"Hil," he whispered, interrupting himself, "did you hear that?"

"What?" Hilary whispered frantically in reply.

"Breathing, like some kind of a big animal. Listen, it's coming from over on your side of the tent."

With a gasp of fear Hilary lunged into her husband's arms, and then frantically she scrambled across him and huddled against him on the opposite side of the tent from where she had been only seconds before. It was only then that she realized that her beloved husband was quietly chuckling.

"You oaf, you made that up!"

"How do you know?" Dwayne laughed quietly. "Listen. I'm sure there's something breathing somewhere out there—"

But he couldn't finish, for once again Dwayne had an attacker going after his ticklish and very vulnerable ribs.

"I remember the other thing my grandparents did on their campout honeymoon," Dwayne said later as he and Hilary lay side by side in the comfortable tent, listening to the wind whip past.

"What was it?"

"They got chased by a rattlesnake."

Hilary raised herself on her elbow. "I'm sure they did, and if your grandfather was as brave as you, he probably beat your grandmother in a footrace down off the mountain."

"Hey, that isn't fair."

"Neither is frightening me with dumb stories, you big lummox."

Dwayne chuckled as his beautiful and imaginative bride leaned and kissed him on the tip of his nose, and then for a long time there was more silence.

"Dwayne?" Hilary finally whispered. "Is there really a cave here that you want to explore?"

"You didn't believe me?"

"I did, but . . . well, you're always teasing."

"I'm not teasing about that cave, Hil. It's here, in this canyon, and I think I may have been the first white man, or boy, to have ever seen it. With a little luck, you'll be the first white woman to see it, too."

Hilary squeezed her husband. "Sounds romantic, sort of like Adam and Eve."

"Yeah," Dwayne replied with a smile. "I hadn't thought of that."

"So, what's so important about this cave? What was in it that so fired your imagination?"

"Perceptive little girl, aren't you! What makes you think something's in the cave?"

"Because I don't think you would come all this way just to see a hole in the ground."

"It's in the wall of the canyon, Hil, not the ground. And you're right, I wouldn't."

"So what's there?"

"We'll let it be a surprise."

"Dwayne!"

"Hey," he laughed, "I like surprises, and you'll learn to like them, too. How do you know it isn't something real valuable, like gold and diamonds and things of that sort? Like you guessed, I've always had a dream of finding a pirate's treasure, or of rolling around in money like the robber barons back east do. Buried treasure! What if that's the surprise I'll be showing you tomorrow? Are you against all money, Hil, or just gambling money?"

Hilary didn't answer, and so, regretting his sarcasm, Dwayne turned to her. "But I don't expect to find a treasure, Hil. Really, I don't. When I was here as a boy, I found several arrowheads and other flint tools just laying around on the floor of the cave. I . . . I've just always wondered if maybe there wasn't something that I missed."

And so the next morning, despite the fact that several inches of snow had fallen—with more threatening—the young couple hiked up the canyon, began a rather steep ascent, and soon found themselves in a strange little cliff-encircled cove.

"It's up there," Dwayne said, pointing up.

"Up that cliff?"

"That's right."

"And you expect me to climb that cliff in these clothes? My word, Dwayne, I'm wearing a dress. It's all I brought with me."

Dwayne smiled and squeezed his wife's shoulder. "Don't worry, Hil. The climb isn't that bad, and the cave isn't very high up there, either."

"But . . . but, Dwayne, the snow has made the rock slick, and now it's starting to snow some more."

This time Dwayne laughed. "Goodness, but you are a worry wart. Now, come on. I'll take care of you."

"Promise?"

Dwayne nodded. So with a sigh, Hilary cautiously followed her husband as he began his climb.

For the next few moments they climbed the water-slick, tortuous wall of cliff, not speaking, and following a trail that wasn't a trail at all. Finally, though snowfall was making visibility difficult, Dwayne found his cave.

"Well, Hil, what do you think?"

Cautiously Hilary looked around her. Actually, she thought, it was not much as far as caves went. It was more just a shallow hole in the side of the cliff, not more than ten or twelve feet deep, and maybe only half that in height.

"It's . . . nice," she finally replied.

"It sure seemed larger when I was a kid," Dwayne said as he also looked around. "And it seemed like there were a ton of arrowheads. But I'll bet, now that I am really trying to remember, that I didn't find more than half a dozen of them. Kick around a little, and let's see if we can find any more of them."

"Uh . . . Dwayne, the snow's getting worse."

"Yeah, I saw."

"Hadn't we ought to start back down?"

Dwayne looked at his wife with a smile. "Getting worried?"

"A little."

"Well, don't. We'll only look around for ten minutes or so, and then we'll be on our way. I . . . say, Hil, look at this! Already I found an arrowhead."

Hilary took the small stone point that Dwayne handed her and absentmindedly examined it. But what she was really thinking of was the steadily falling snow. What if one of them should fall when descending the cliffs? The thought was frightening, and Hilary could not get it out of her head.

"Dwayne," she said when nearly an hour more had passed, "we'd better go."

Looking up, Dwayne smiled his winning smile again. "You're right, Hil. And I'm ready. I only found eleven points, but they are dandies, all of them. There's a fellow in Denver who will pay me good money for these, so the trip has certainly been worthwhile."

"Are you sure that you should take them?"

Dwayne laughed. "Of course I'm sure. The Indians who left them here don't want them anymore, I can tell you that."

"But maybe this land belongs to someone."

"Finders, keepers, Hil. You know the old saying. Now listen, why don't I go first, and you come after me. That way I can test the trail."

And that was the way they started back down the cliff, Dwayne feeling his way, and Hilary following after, doing her best to use the same handholds and footholds as had her husband. But the snow had made the rocks treacherous, not only because they had become slick but also because the snow hid dangerous places that might otherwise have been obvious.

"You doing all right?" Dwayne called up when they had descended about halfway.

"I . . . I think so," Hilary gasped. "But these new shoes are so slick!"

"Just be careful, Hil."

"I am. I wish I had moccasins, though, and this darn dress keeps me from seeing—"

Suddenly Hilary's foot slipped from a toehold she had found, and as she slid she grasped for a root, which turned out to be only a dead limb which had fallen to that point earlier. With a cry she tried to warn Dwayne, urging him to catch her. But then she was past him, sliding, falling.

Dwayne, startled, looked up only in time to see his wife hurtle past. He started to put out one arm to stop her, but the weight of her body knocked it aside, and in horror he watched as Hilary plummeted thirty feet or so down the hill. Twice he saw her hit; the first time she hit ended her scream. A second or two later, when her body came to rest at the base of the cliff and lay still, Dwayne heard his own scream tearing out of his throat.

Frantically he scrambled down the cliff and knelt beside his wife's still form. She was breathing, but it was obvious that her right leg had been broken, and no matter what he did, Dwayne could not bring her out of unconsciousness.

Picking her up, he made his way out of the cove and, with great difficulty, down the next slope and back to his new Pierce Arrow touring car.

After brushing the snow from the seat, Dwayne arranged Hilary as well as he could, packing blankets and the tent around her to both keep her warm and to hold her in place. Then, frantically, he cranked the automobile's engine until it clattered to life. Still Hilary did not move, and almost sobbing with fear, Dwayne scrambled behind the wheel and began forcing the vehicle forward, down the snow-covered, rock-strewn trail that led back into Ogden Canyon.

The road, terribly rough the afternoon before, was now made treacherous with the still-falling snow. Nevertheless, Dwayne did his best to hurry, forcing the costly new vehicle indiscriminately over logs and boulders and whatever else might be in his path.

And he was making good time, too, until the left front tire slammed into a sharp-edged boulder and exploded with a loud bang. Stopping the car with a curse, Dwayne leaped out and examined the damage. The tire was shot, and to drive on the rim would destroy both it and the spoked wheel. His other tire had gone flat the afternoon before, and he had not taken time to find a repair kit.

Glancing at Hilary, Dwayne was shocked at how white her face had grown since he had placed her on the seat. Scrambling around the car, Dwayne felt her wrist and could find only the faintest of pulses. Pulling back the blankets he could see that her leg, where it had fractured, was swelling badly, and the bone looked as if it were about to burst through the skin.

Frantically he repositioned the blankets, and then, his breath coming in sobs, he thought of giving his beloved wife a blessing. But when he put his hands on her head to do so, he had a terrible feeling of guilt, almost as if . . . as if . . .

"Dear God," he wept as he stood in the steadily falling snow, "I . . . I can't do it! I feel so confounded guilty that I don't think my prayer would even get through the clouds. Please take my guilt away, Heavenly Father, so I can feel good about giving my wife a blessing."

But the feeling persisted, and so with a cry of frustration Dwayne dropped his hands and ran back to the other side of the car. Jamming it in gear, he pulled the throttle, and, ignoring the damage that he knew was occurring to the left front wheel, he started again down the road.

"Heavenly Father," he prayed as he drove, "I know I'm not very righteous. Maybe Hilary was right, and I . . . I'm too concerned about worldly things. But oh, dear God, Hilary isn't that way! You know her, dear Heavenly Father. She's worthy to be blessed, even if I'm not worthy to bless her. Please, dear God, bless her, and . . . and I swear, I will do my best to be less worldly. Now, please bless this car that it will get us down into Ogden."

Suddenly the steering wheel was wrenched violently to the side, and with a feeling of helplessness Dwayne felt the car follow, almost in slow motion, until it finally slammed into some boulders and tipped onto its side.

For a moment Dwayne lay in the snow, trying to understand what had happened. But then his mind focused, and he realized that he was beneath his wife's unconscious form.

"Hilary," he gasped as he worked his way out from beneath her. "Hil, please hear me!"

But the unconscious woman didn't respond.

"God," Dwayne suddenly shouted as he kicked at the overturned automobile, "why did you do this to me? To us! What kind of God are you!"

Sitting down in the snow, then, and cradling his wife's head in his arms, Dwayne lowered his face into his wife's still, white countenance and began to sob. He was no longer praying, nor was he making any more vain promises. He was simply holding her, loving her, knowing finally that he had lost her, and knowing, too, that it was a loss greater than he could begin to comprehend.

What did cars, money, fine properties, and numerous servants matter? Of what value were position and prestige and other such things if he didn't have his beloved Hilary there to share them with him?

Worse, his mind screamed at him, might he have lost her in the hereafter, as well? If his guilt for past sins was so great that he couldn't even give his wife a blessing, then surely he wouldn't be worthy of having the sealing ordinances of the temple take effect in their marriage.

Greater and more wracking sobs followed, and for long, agonizing moments Dwayne tried to deal with that. But no peace came, not even when he began praying again, praying with greater earnestness than he had prayed since during his mission.

Finally, his emotions spent, Dwayne rose to his feet, picked up the still form of his wife, and began hobbling down the trail. He moved as though drunken, and he also moved without hope, though his mind could not seem to stop praying, pleading.

"Say, mister? What's the trouble?"

Startled, Dwayne looked up to see an old man and a younger one seated on the seat of a two-horse wagon.

"It's . . . it's my wife," Dwayne gasped as he tried to comprehend. "She's hurt bad."

"And you figure on carrying her all the way to Ogden?" the older man asked.

"I . . . I don't have a choice."

"You do now. Brother Jim, help him lift her into the wagon whilst I arrange these blankets."

Quickly the younger man leaped down, and gently he and Dwayne placed Hilary's still form in the bed of the wagon.

"Thank you," Dwayne gasped. "I . . . I . . . say, did that fellow call you brother?"

"He did."

"Are you . . . Mormons?"

"We are."

"Sir, uh . . . Hilary needs a blessing badly, and . . . well, I'm not exactly worthy."

"And you hope that we are?"

Dwayne nodded.

"Well, brother, we're both trying to be, I'll say that. Here, put your hands on her head with old Ben's and mine," the young man said gently. "She needs your strength, too. Now, you say her name is Hilary?"

And so the blessing was given. And though the snow continued to fall with greater and greater power, Dwayne, seated in the back of the bouncing wagon with his unconscious wife, could not stop smiling through his tears. For his dear Hilary had been promised by the power of the priesthood that she would live. And that meant that she, and he, could go to work together on repenting and then building Christ's kingdom.

Thursday, November 3, 1910

Randolph, Utah

The cold front we have been following is traveling very slowly as it moves parallel with the jet stream across northern Utah. The storm seems to have settled into place, with whipping winds and pelting snow being the lot of all who live in the area. More significantly, the cold front now develops what scientists today call a Williams Wave.

The Williams Wave, a small low-pressure system that appears like a wave on the relatively straight line of a stalled cold front, was named after meteorologist Phil Williams, who discovered that storms with such waves bring the heaviest snow into northern Utah. Caused when a surge in the jet stream (a jet max) creates a surface low pressure along a stalled cold front, this developing low-pressure system then moves northeast along the stalled front and underneath the polar jet stream, bringing about more than usual precipitation. The heaviest snowfall is usually in a narrow strip twenty-five to thirty miles wide that follows just north of the jet stream.

In the case of the storm we have been following, the wave roars like a freight train along the stalled front as it crosses the Wasatch Mountains northeast of Ogden, accompanied by heavy snow and high winds, bringing a severe early winter to the farming valleys of northern Utah.

This is particularly significant to a ranching family who have been undergoing a fairly difficult situation.

HEDGING UP THE WAY

Duff Wilkey sat at the table in his kitchen on Otter Creek, just five miles north of Randolph, Utah. It was a nice kitchen, too —warm, light, and comfortable, with large southern windows to let in the sun; and modern, with running water from the spring out back, a new wood-burning stove, and all the other conveniences that the Sears, Roebuck and Company catalog could provide. Yes, Duff had done well with his large ranch, and he had tried to use what he had been blessed with to make life easier for his wife, Miranda, his sweetheart of thirty-seven years.

Now he looked at her again, still pretty as a picture, busy ladling hot water from the stove's reservoir so that she could clean up the dishes. That was his beloved Andy, all right— busy, busy, busy. So far as he had ever been able to discover, she didn't have a "relax" bone in her body. The very concept seemed foreign to her. She went hard from the crack of dawn until she fell into bed at night, and then she slept the sleep of angels because she so thoroughly deserved it.

Duff thought of that, thought of his own inclination to work and to rest hard, and smiled. He couldn't bear doing nothing at all. But on the other hand, he *could* spend hours reading the scriptures, and hours more simply thinking, praying, and pondering on what he had read. To poor, dear Andy it looked as if he were being the laziest man in the world, but Duff simply didn't agree with her. As far as he was concerned, it was time well spent. Such hours alone with the Lord and his thoughts had helped him to be successful in his numerous Church callings, had helped him to sort out some peculiar genealogical problems in his family line, and had helped him greatly in developing his ranch. They had also helped him to successfully assist Andy in rearing their nine living children.

Well, eight had been successfully reared. The ninth, twenty-year-old Maggie, was suddenly becoming a sort of problem. Even as he sat there he could hear her upstairs, her crying sobs almost keeping rhythm with the Regulator clock in the hallway.

"Quite a storming blowing up," he said as he glanced outside. "I'm thankfuller'n somewhat that Joe and I got those cattle down off the upper pastures early this year."

Miranda looked sharply at her husband. "Don't change the subject on me, Duff Wilkey. I want to know what you did."

Duff stretched back, his hands locked behind his head, and placed his stockinged feet up on the chair before him. Then he smiled peacefully.

"Duff, I mean it."

"I know you do," he replied softly. "And, as I already told you, Andy, I used the priesthood. I knelt in prayer and pronounced a blessing on this whole marriage affair that nothing that was displeasing to Heavenly Father would occur until both you and I could obtain peace about it, and until Maggie could see the entire picture."

Miranda scowled. "That's a *blessing?* You'll have to explain yourself a little better than that, Duff."

"Then sit down, Andy, and look at me when I'm talking. I can hardly abide talking to somebody's backside, even if that somebody is as attractive as you."

"Oh, pshaw!" Miranda said with a smile as she came and sat at the table. "You cut out the blarney, Duff Wilkey, and tell me exactly what you did upstairs last night."

"To get the record straight," Duff finally began, "let's start way back. You remember when Jamie didn't come home with the cattle that night ten, eleven years ago?"

"I do. It was an awful night."

"It was. Remember as we knelt in prayer, both of us had the feeling that he had been hurt?"

Miranda nodded.

"Do you remember what we did about it, Andy?"

"I certainly do. You pronounced a priesthood blessing on him that he would be protected and preserved until we could find him, determine the problem, and then help him."

Duff nodded. "You've a good memory, Andy. Well, last night while I was praying, I got to thinking on that blessing I gave Jamie. I hadn't thought of it in years, but in an instant it all came back to me, every word. So I asked the Lord if he had brought that memory into my mind, and I felt very strongly that he had. So I asked why."

"And?"

"And the next thing I knew, Jamie was gone from my mind and I was thinking of Maggie and Budge Morgan and of pronouncing a blessing on their relationship."

Miranda shook her head. "You're an interesting man, Duff

Wilkey. Of all things—blessing a relationship. For the life of me I don't know how you come up with these ideas."

Duff grinned mischievously. "Clean living, Andy, pure and simple."

"Humph!"

"Humph yourself. But I'll give you this, Andy. I've never read of such a thing in the scriptures, and I've never heard any of the Brethren speak of it. All I know is that I had the definite impression to do what I did, and I was obedient to my impression."

Miranda nodded. "Well, Duff, the proof will be in the pudding, as they say. But you're sure you did the right thing?"

Duff smiled. "All right, Andy, so that you will stop worrying, I'll go into more detail. But you asked for it, so you'll have to bear with me. This past July 10, according to my journal, the Lord gave me a dream, warning me that Maggie was either in or was going to be in some great danger. You remember me telling you of the dream?"

"I do."

"Good. That night I talked to Maggie—sort of interviewed her, I guess—and so far as either of us could tell, nothing in her life was amiss. So I took the problem before the Lord and had the impression then that the danger was future, not present. We've spoken of this, too."

Miranda nodded briskly, as if to hurry her husband along, "Yes, we have. Go on, please."

"Be patient, Andy," Duff said as he held up his hand in a peace gesture. "I'm going over all this again as much for my own benefit as for yours. Now, correct me if I get any of this fouled up. Two weeks later, on July 24, Mags came home from the celebration in town all aglow with excitement because of the young man she had met and spent the afternoon with. That was the first any of us had ever heard of Budge Morgan."

"And I was relieved," Andy stated firmly. "No boy had given Maggie more than a day's worth of excitement in over a year—since Joel's death—and I was thrilled to see that blush in her cheeks again."

"I remember you saying that," Duff responded. "I think I even felt the same. Then the next morning, July 25, I had another dream. In that dream, my grandfather was standing next to me, instructing me to watch out for Maggie. Then I was shown a picture of two young people. When I prayed about what I had seen, the feeling I had was that Grandfather had warned me that Maggie's danger would come in the form of a beau—maybe Budge Morgan.

"Well, by the end of the week, Budge was all Mags could talk about. It was 'Budge this,' or 'Budge that,' or 'Budge something else.' It was obvious to me that she was quite rapidly falling in love. That was confirmed when Maggie came home about two weeks after their first date and announced that she was engaged to be married."

"That was when you expressed your concern to her."

"That's right, Andy. It was also when Maggie, rather defiantly, I might add, challenged us to pray and see what the Lord had to say about her and Budge."

"Which we did."

"That's right. And we both felt a withdrawal of the Spirit when we asked if the Lord approved of Budge as her husband."

Miranda nodded solemnly. "Maggie certainly didn't like what we had to tell her."

"Whoo-eee," Duff exclaimed softly. "That's an understatement, Andy. I've never seen her so upset with us. When she told us we were trying to stand between her and happiness, I came closer to bawling like a young calf than I have in years."

"I know you did, Duff. I saw it in your face. But I don't think she ever meant to hurt us."

"Of course she didn't, Andy. She was just in pain herself. But I decided then that I had to learn all I could about Budge Morgan and maybe help her that way if I couldn't sway her opinion by spiritual information alone."

"But Budge had been in our home several times," Miranda said softly. "We all liked him, Duff, and really enjoyed his personality."

Duff nodded. "I know. He was active in the Church, had served a mission in the South, and I remember the night when he told us that he wanted a temple marriage. It all sounded wonderful, but I couldn't get rid of this squirrelly feeling I had every time I prayed about him. So, I started asking questions."

"Not too discreetly, I might add."

Duff acknowledged his wife's gentle rebuke. "I know, and

I am truly sorry about that. I didn't mean for word to get back to Maggie that I was going around the country asking questions about her fiancé."

"She thought it was just one more indication that you didn't trust her."

"I know she did, Andy. She yelled at me that night after she had learned I had been digging around a little. I know now that I really hurt her feelings, and as it turned out, it wasn't worth it. Not only did I not learn one blamed thing that was negative about Budge but it also turned Maggie more toward him than ever."

Miranda nodded vigorously. "That's no fooling. The very next day she marched in with the news that she and Budge would be getting married in October—day after tomorrow, to be exact. Your meddling pushed her into hurrying things up, for a fact."

Duff smiled sadly. "You're right, Andy. I've apologized a hundred times for it, and I'll probably be apologizing for the rest of my life, the way memories in this family seem to hang on. But on the other hand, I don't feel entirely at fault. Twice in dreams the Lord had warned me concerning my baby daughter, and every prayer I ever offered after she had asked me to find out from the Lord what she should do, I felt the Spirit's withdrawal when I asked if the Lord approved of Maggie marrying Budge. So I had to do something, and it seemed logical to begin with learning all I could about him."

"Which didn't work."

"Well, not like I had expected. I did learn that he was born in Logan and that at the moment he is living in Kemmerer, Wyoming. He is LDS, did serve a mission to the South, and was here in Randolph on July 24 visiting one of his missionary companions, Charlie Fellows, who seems to think quite highly of him."

"Not great recommendations for all your negative feelings," Miranda observed dryly.

"Amen. Which is exactly why, suspicioning my own inspiration, I finally sent you last week to the temple over in Logan. I wanted you to either get another confirmation of the same things that I was feeling or to find out from the Lord that both of us had somehow been misled. So far as I have been able to learn, there is no better place on earth for receiving guidance and revelation than in the Lord's holy temple."

Now Miranda sighed. "I'll tell you the truth, Duff. I hate this mess!"

"I know, Andy. So do I!"

Miranda stood and walked to the counter, where she stared out of the window at the blowing snow. "I'll tell you something else. In all the years we've been married, Duff, I've never doubted your inspiration—that is, not until you told me the first time that Maggie wasn't supposed to marry Budge. Then, seeing how happy she seemed, I doubted."

"And now?"

Slowly Miranda turned to face her husband. "You know what happened at the temple, Duff. I've already told you every detail of it. Suffice it to say that I feel just as certain as you that Maggie shouldn't marry that man."

"Not, at least," Duff added softly, "if she wants to avoid all sorts of heartaches. When I was praying the morning you left for Logan, the Lord showed me in my mind what her marriage to him would be like. I suppose you could call it a sort of vision, it was so real.

"Whatever it was, I saw Maggie in a home that I have never seen before. She had two or three tiny children, and when she opened the door to me, I had never seen such agony and grief as I saw on her face. It was awful! Instantly she started crying, pleading with me to take her home, and she was still pleading when the scene sort of faded out on me. I'm telling you, Andy, I can't get that picture out of my mind."

Soberly Miranda nodded. "I believe you, Duff. The trouble is, Maggie doesn't. What are we supposed to do about that?"

Helplessly Duff shrugged his shoulders. "Nothing we can do, Andy, except exercise our faith that the Lord will heed our prayers, including the blessing I pronounced last night, and pull off some sort of miracle that will stop the wedding. Maybe this snowstorm is it."

"But that won't do any good," Miranda argued, "not in the long run. Oh, it may slow things down for a day or so, but it certainly won't change anything. Not as far as Maggie is concerned, it won't."

"I know that," Duff responded quietly. "And I don't know what else to say. I've done what I felt directed by the Spirit to do so that the marriage will be stopped until we can all learn what is going on, and now I guess we can only wait—wait to see what the Lord intends to do for our daughter."

Miranda shook her head. "But, Duff," she argued, "the wedding is only two days away, Budge is supposed to be here tonight, and . . . and . . . well, there's simply nothing else that we can do to stop it!"

And with that awful thought, Miranda finally broke into tears.

"I see you have her crying, too."

The statement, made by Maggie as she descended the stairs and interrupted their conversation, was intended to hurt Duff. He knew that and was wise enough to understand that his daughter was still lashing out because she herself was suffering so deeply. So he didn't respond.

Maggie stepped to the window, where she looked anxiously out at the mounting blizzard. For a long moment she stood silently, and then, her back still to her parents, she finally spoke again.

"And like Mother, Daddy, I would like to know what you think you did that will stop my marriage to Budge. Because whatever it was, I can guarantee you that it won't work!"

Spinning, Maggie then faced her parents, her tear-reddened eyes flashing defiance and anger. "When Budge gets here, I'm going with him. And as far as I am concerned, I don't care if I never see either one of you again—the whole rest of my life!"

"Maggie, you don't mean that," Miranda pleaded.

"Oh, no? Just you watch and see what I mean. I just can't stand this feeling you're giving me. You don't trust me! You don't even care about me! Why should I care about you anymore?"

For several moments there was silence in the room, broken only by the ticking of the Regulator clock, the crackle of wood burning in the stove, and the moaning of the wind outside. Duff Wilkey, at a loss to know what to say, traced his fingers across the checkered pattern on the oilcloth that covered the table. Miranda sat across from him, gazing at her daughter, her eyes pleading eloquently for Maggie to listen to their concerns.

"Well, Daddy?" Maggie finally demanded. "What do you have to say for yourself?"

"Please sit down, Mags," Duff gently replied.

"What for?"

Duff forced himself to smile a little. "You did ask me to respond to a question you and your mother have both asked, didn't you? I'll be happy to do so, but that old crick in my neck is hurting today, and it'd surely be easier on me if I could speak to you without having to look up."

Maggie hesitated, and then finally took a chair next to her

mother. "So, what did you do?" she asked again, her eyes riveted past Duff and on the window.

"I pronounced a priesthood blessing on you and Budge."

"You what?"

"I said, Mags, that I pronounced a priesthood blessing—to hedge up the way of your relationship so that if it is not according to the Lord's will, your marriage to Budge Morgan will be prevented until we can all learn the truth about it."

"Daddy," Maggie said as new tears started down her cheeks, "you had no right to do that! Oh, why did you do it? Why?"

"No right, Mags? Are you sure you know what you are talking about?"

"Of course, I do," Maggie responded as she angrily wiped her eyes with her arm. "Daddy, I'm not a little girl anymore, you know! I'm an adult, and I am entitled to make these decisions on my own. Do you know what's wrong with you and Mother? You . . . you're just afraid of losing the last of your children, and of being alone here. But you can't hold on to me anymore! I have a right to my own life, and I have a right to my own inspiration. In case you can't remember, that's called free agency."

Duff nodded. "I believe in agency, Mags, and I can see how you would feel this way. But you need to understand that nowhere in the scriptures is it ever called free. It is simply called *agency*, and if you will study it, you will see that a price is always associated with it—the price of obedience. Without obedience, one immediately becomes bound by the consequences of one's disobedient decisions. And even though agency still prevails, it cannot alter the consequences of our decisions. This is called the law of justice."

"So? What does that have to do with me? I've been obedient. All my life I've kept the commandments. I have done practically everything you ever asked of me, besides."

"I know that, Mags, and Mother and I love and honor you for it. Still, agency and the price we pay for it has everything to do with all of us in this room. Now, you asked why I used my priesthood in your behalf, and I'm going to tell you. But I won't do it until you have settled down, stopped being angry, and are willing to listen."

"I *am* listening!" Maggie stormed. "But if you're going to tell me about your stupid dreams again, or about your supposed answers to prayer, or about Mother going to the temple and feeling that I shouldn't marry Budge, then forget it! I already know all that, and I'm sick of hearing it. I've prayed too, you know. I have a right to get my own answer about marrying Budge, and I've got it! I feel good about what I am doing, and you won't be able to stop me, priesthood or not."

Duff reached back and rubbed his neck where it was hurting. "I won't even try to stop you, Mags," he replied gently. "If your Mother's and my impressions are accurate, then the Lord will heed the blessing I pronounced, and your marriage won't occur. He'll stop it himself until all this is resolved. If we should happen to be wrong, however, then because of the blessing I pronounced last night, and believe me, I chose my words carefully, the Lord will hedge up your mother's and my way so that we won't be able to prevent your eternal happiness, and you can go ahead and be married as planned."

"You . . . you said that?" Maggie asked, sounding absolutely dumbfounded.

"I did."

"I . . . I didn't know that the priesthood could be used like that."

"I didn't either," Duff responded softly. "At least not until last night, when I was praying. Then it felt to me like the Holy Ghost put into my mind how to do what I did, and even the words to use."

"How . . . how come I've never heard of this . . . this 'hedging up the way' stuff!"

Duff shook his head. "I don't know, Mags. I hadn't ever heard of it, either, at least in this context. But after my prayer, I got out the scriptures and located several references where the Lord uses the phrase, hedging up the way. In Hosea, chapter 2, verse 6, it is mentioned, and three times in the Book of Mormon it is used. Twice it seems to be a spiritual thing, as in 2 Nephi, chapter 4, verse 33, where Nephi is pleading with the Lord that he not hedge up Nephi's way but instead hedge up the way of Nephi's enemies, and again in Mosiah, chapter 7, verse 29, where the Lord promises to hedge up the way of his iniquitous people so that they will not be allowed to prosper. Then in Ether, chapter 9, verse 33, the Lord states that he hedged up the way of the ancient Jaredites with serpents. Finally, Mags, the Lord told Joseph Smith in the Doctrine and Covenants, section 122, verse 7, that no matter what things combined to hedge up his way, they would all give him experience and would be for his good."

"So what does all that have to do with me?"

"Nothing, and everything. While none of these scriptures were given to you personally by the Lord, they point out very clearly that the concept of hedging up the way is not something I made up last night."

"They also point out, Daddy, that it is the Lord who hedges up the way, and not some mortal like yourself!"

Duff smiled. "Of course, you're right. And that should give you some comfort, Mags."

"But . . . but *you* did it."

"Mags, honey, I bless people when they are ill, too. But who is it who heals them when they are made well?"

"The Lord," Maggie responded quietly.

"Exactly. And who is it, no matter what I have said, who decides whether they are to be healed."

Maggie sighed deeply. "The Lord."

"Correct again. That's why I always end a blessing with the phrase, 'if it be the Lord's will.' I want the final decision left up to the Lord, not me. By the same token, though I was the voice of the prayer and blessing last night, Heavenly Father makes the decision about any hedging up of the way of your marriage. Whatever is done will be according to his divine will, not mine."

"So . . . maybe . . . I will still marry Budge?" Maggie asked hopefully.

"Very definitely—if we are wrong. That is your agency that you spoke of. But you should know, Mags, that I don't think we are wrong."

"In which case I lose my agency," Maggie declared with frustration. "It doesn't seem fair that somebody else controls my agency."

"Nobody but you will ever control your agency, Mags. We wouldn't attempt to stop you from doing what you really wanted, and Heavenly Father never will, either. In fact, he lost one third of his children in premortality because they didn't like the law of agency and the responsibility that comes with it, so they rebelled against it and him. But because agency was so important, Father had to let them rebel, which cost them everything, as you know. Even now Heavenly Father continues to lose children for the same reason —they choose to leave him.

"In the short run, though, you asked us to pray about whether you should marry Budge. We did, told you what we had felt, and then watched as you rejected our counsel.

Therefore, fearing for you and doing my best to respond to the promptings of the Holy Ghost, I exercised the law of stewardship—I *am* your mortal father, you remember. In that sense, by pronouncing that blessing, I did sort of temporarily remove your agency. I guess that sometimes maybe the one law overlaps the other."

"How do you mean?"

"Well, in doing what I did, I asked Heavenly Father to alter conditions so that the marriage, if there is something unrighteous about it or about any of the parties involved, will be stopped, or hedged up, until such time as we can all understand why Mother and I have been having such negative feelings about it. To that extent, if we are right, then somehow you will be prevented from marrying Budge at the appointed time."

"It's probably you that caused this miserable storm," Maggie said then, her sarcasm obvious.

"Maggie," Miranda said, speaking for the first time, "please don't speak like that. Your father can't cause storms, and you know it."

"But Heavenly Father can."

"That's true. And if he did cause the storm in order to hedge up the way of your marriage, that means it must be pretty important to him that you not marry Budge."

"What . . . do you mean?"

"I mean," Miranda said softly, "that normally Heavenly Father lets us make all the mistakes we want to make. Then he allows us to suffer as we learn from them. That's one way his children grow spiritually. But this must be a special case, Mags, a situation that would be so tragic for you, or for Budge, that Father desires it to be stopped. How else can you explain the dreams and impressions that both your father and I have had? I assume they mean that this particular marriage would have negative eternal implications not only for one or both of you but also for others. In other words, marrying Budge would hurt not only you but perhaps also generations of other people. That was certainly the impression I received last week in the temple."

"You . . . didn't tell me that."

"Honey, lately you haven't let me tell you much of anything."

"There's something else, Mags," Duff added gently. "The other reason that Heavenly Father told your mother and me what he did is that he loves you dearly. You are a righteous young woman, and so you are worthy of his protection. Your mother and I are truly thankful that the Lord has blessed us with such a wonderful daughter, and we're real thankful that he cares so much about you."

For a moment all sat still, silently listening as the wind moaned against the sturdy house. "That's all well and good," Maggie said finally. "But I still don't understand why I can't get my own answers to prayer. I mean, we're taught to do that, aren't we?"

"We are," Duff responded, "and you are entitled. But Mags, to my understanding, this is where the law of stewardship comes into play."

"Daddy, I'm an adult! Don't I have stewardship over my *own* life?"

"I know you're an adult, Mags. And of course you have stewardship over yourself. But the way you're talking, I must have missed the meeting."

"Meeting?" Maggie asked, looking confused. "What meeting?"

"The one where I was released as your father, and where Andy was released as your mother."

Maggie smiled thinly at her father's humor. "Daddy, come on."

"I'm really not trying to be funny, Mags. No matter how old you get, we will never lose our stewardship as your parents. Besides that, at the moment, and until you are actually married to a worthy priesthood holder, I am also your direct priesthood leader. When I feel that the Lord is speaking to me concerning the fact that you are not to marry Budge, or anything else regarding you and your life, then I have the responsibility to act upon it and to inform you of these impressions—even if it is very uncomfortable for me to do so. That is my stewardship. This is especially true when you come to me and ask me to go before the Lord seeking divine counsel in your behalf. In that situation, we have both exercised our agency.

"Your stewardship at that point, Mags, is to go before the Lord and ask for a confirmation of what I have told you. If you seek an opposite revelation, or even your own special answer, then you are ignoring my stewardship and may possibly be deceived."

"But . . . but how do you know that?"

"Because of the scriptures, Mags, which contain examples of that very thing. For instance, when Lehi told his family about his dream of the tree of life, some rebelled, some accepted, and sweet, righteous Nephi went out alone before the Lord, where he asked for a confirmation of what had been shown his father.

"Pleased with the young man's faith and righteous attitude, the Lord showed Nephi the same scene, and then elaborated on it, which is the Lord's privilege.

"Another example is when Lehi had a dream that directed his sons to return to Jerusalem to obtain the brass plates. As you remember, Nephi treated that message as if it had come to him directly from the Lord instead of roundabout through his father. A third example of this righteous attitude occured when Nephi went to his father and asked where he should go to hunt meat for their hungry family, despite the fact that, at the moment, Nephi was definitely more worthy of revelation than his father was.

"What we are to learn from these accounts, Mags, is simple. When your priesthood leader speaks to you of a message from the Lord, your response should be to accept it as such, and then to go before the Lord asking for a confirmation or rejection of your leader's words."

"And if I get a rejection?"

"Then you come back to your priesthood leader and tell him of your impressions. Then both of you can work together to find out why there is a discrepancy."

"How do you know that isn't what happened to me?"

"Is it?" Miranda asked gently. "Mags, have you asked for a confirmation of what your father and I told you?"

Slowly Maggie shook her head.

"Then maybe it's the moment for you to do that," Miranda said softly, "before much more time passes."

And with this suggestion, the conversation came to a close.

By late afternoon, Budge Morgan still hadn't arrived, and Maggie was growing more nervous by the minute. The storm had only grown worse, and the snow was blowing and drifting so badly that the barn and other outbuildings had virtually disappeared in the whiteout.

In the Wilkey home, however, the kitchen was warm and snug, and all three members of the family were gathered there. They were all silent, however, almost in awe of the fierceness of the out-of-season blizzard that raged outside.

"Did you hear that?" Duff suddenly said as he sat up straight in his chair. "Blamed if I didn't hear what sounded like a voice."

"Budge!" Maggie screamed, and with a rush she was into her coat and scarf.

"Mags," Duff growled as he struggled into his boots. "Please don't you go out there alone—"

But Maggie was gone out the door, screaming Budge's name, and it was another minute or two before Duff could follow her.

"Maggie?" he called as he stepped into the snow and wind. "Maggie, where are you?"

Duff could not hear an answer, but Maggie's boot tracks led around toward the front of the house, directly into the teeth of the storm. Bowing his head, he followed, and seconds later nearly stumbled over Maggie and another person when he rounded the corner of the house.

"Daddy," Maggie shouted frantically, "she needs help."

Struggling, Duff and Maggie carried the bundled form of a woman back to the door and into the kitchen. There Miranda took over, and Duff went back out to see to the woman's team and wagon.

When the horses were finally in his barn and feeding in a couple of empty stalls, and when he had hurriedly completed his evening chores, Duff made his way back into the house.

"Well," he said as he gazed at the blanket-shrouded woman, "you look some better already."

The woman, who, now that he could see her, turned out to be hardly more than a girl, nodded her head. But her teeth were still chattering so that she could hardly talk, and so Duff didn't push it. He did learn, however, that she had been traveling alone, so he stopped worrying that there were others still out in the blizzard. But still he was worried plenty, for not even Maggie had any idea who the young woman might be.

An hour later, after constant chitchat about nothing at all by both Maggie and Miranda as they ministered to the girl's needs, Duff laid down his latest issue of the *Utah Genealogical and Historical Magazine*. "Girl," he then said with a smile, "you do look some better."

"Her name is Jane, Daddy."

"Oh," Duff said with a raise of his brows. "How'd I miss that?"

"You were reading," Miranda said as if that explained everything. "Duff, this is Miss Jane Kirkwood. She is from Kemmerer and was on her way to Logan."

"All that way alone?" Duff asked in surprise.

Jane nodded silently.

"We're some south of Sage Creek Junction," Duff then observed. "You're a little off the road to Logan."

"I . . . I got lost in the storm, I suppose," she responded quietly. "I don't even remember a junction. I . . . I just let the horses go when I couldn't see the road anymore, and they . . . brought me here."

"Smartest thing you could have done," Miranda declared with motherly solicitation as she pushed another cup of hot milk before the girl. "My husband has returned home safely several times just by letting his horses have their heads. Isn't that so, dear?"

"Well, once or twice, maybe."

"Pshaw, Duff. You fess up and tell the girl."

Duff smiled. "All right. Several it must be. Now, Jane, what were you doing out in a mess like this?"

"I . . . I have to get to Logan."

"Must be pretty all-fired urgent."

"It is. But it wasn't even snowing when I left home. This storm sort of caught me by surprise . . . and . . . and . . ."

Jane was suddenly crying, and Duff sat there helplessly, wondering why every woman in his life had to be crying on that one particular day.

"I . . . I'm sorry," Jane finally said as she got her emotions a little under control. "I . . . I . . . Well, phooey on these old tears! I don't have time for them anyway. Tell me, how soon do you think I can be on my way?"

"Merciful heavens, girl!" Miranda stormed while Duff and Maggie simply stared in amazement. "Until this storm ends, you'll be going nowhere."

"But I must get to Logan!"

"What is it that can be so serious?" Duff finally asked.

Slowly the girl dropped her gaze. "It's . . . it's a personal matter. I just . . . well . . . now for certain I'll be too late."

And with that Jane burst into more tears.

While Miranda comforted her, Maggie walked to the window where she stared out into the gathering darkness. "Daddy," she said worriedly, "do you think he's okay?"

Helplessly Duff shrugged his shoulders. "I don't know, honey. He's a smart feller, though, so I assume he's found a warm hole somewhere to crawl into. Was it me, I sure would have."

"So . . . you don't think I should expect him tonight?"

"In this blizzard, Mags? Not on your life! That Miss Jane Kirkwood here got this far is a pure miracle. Since he was due hours ago, then I assume your beau left hours earlier than Jane. No, if he was coming, he'd have been here long before now."

"Jane," Maggie asked as she turned back toward the room, "did you pass anyone on the road. From Kemmerer, I mean?"

"I didn't," Jane answered quietly. "I was hoping to pass him, but—"

"*Him?*" Duff questioned, his interest suddenly piqued. "Were you expecting to meet somebody, Jane?"

The girl, terribly embarrassed, did not respond, and suddenly Duff laughed out loud. "By jings," he declared, "you were running away to get yourself married, weren't you!"

Jane's eyes grew wide with surprise, and then vigorously she shook her head and rose to her feet. "That isn't so. I would never—"

"Then why were you expecting to meet a man on the road?" Duff pressed, insistently but not unkindly. "Jane, we're your friends here, and we understand kids itching to get married. Andy and I have gone through those portals eight times now and have just one left to go, if we can manage to pull it off."

"Daddy!"

"Sorry, Mags. Jane, how old are you?"

"Seventeen."

"Seventeen," Miranda exclaimed. "Jane, child, do your folks know where you are?"

"Pa's dead," the girl responded. "But Ma knows. I told her I was coming, and she gave me her blessing."

"But to get married? Merciful heavens, child, you're too young—"

"I told you already," Jane declared forcefully. "I am *not* running away to get married!"

"Then what?"

"If you must know," the young girl said with a sigh as she sat back down, looking suddenly very tired, "I am trying to stop one."

Now Duff and Miranda looked at each other, finally understanding that their young visitor was emotionally disturbed. How, they were asking themselves, could a seventeen-year-old girl, alone in a blizzard, possibly expect to be thinking clearly? That was what the Wilkeys were thinking, and that was what they continued to think—at least for another moment.

But Maggie wasn't thinking like Duff and Miranda, not at all. Suddenly she was way ahead of her parents, and questions were building in her mind more rapidly than she could form them into words.

"Jane," she asked hesitantly, "are . . . are you going to . . . to have a . . . a baby?"

"Me?" Jane responded with surprise. "My word, no! Whatever gave you that dumb idea?"

But Maggie, relief in her face, sank back into her own chair without answering.

"It isn't me I'm worried about," Jane went on, her eyes no longer seeing the family but instead looking off into some great distance. "My big sister's the one who's . . . well, I'm doing this for her. She was supposed to be getting married, but then she got real sick and things sort of fell apart. Next thing we knew, we heard about some girl over in Cokeville who was also engaged to be married to my sis's beau. Then a couple of nights ago she found a letter to her beau from another girl, here in Utah, talking all about this other girl's upcoming marriage to him. That's three girls this dandy is engaged to be married to, pretty much all at one time.

"Yesterday, the girl over in Cokeville came to see my sister, and I guess she admitted to some pretty deplorable things that she and my sis's beau had done. My sis won't tell me about them, but I think they must have been, well, *compromising* is the word my ma used.

"Now he's all set to marry this girl from here in Utah. And I . . . I just can't let that happen to someone, even if I don't know her.

"So last night my sis and my ma and me, we all got to talking about how it wasn't right that a dandy like him should desecrate God's holy temple. Billy isn't a good person, not today anyway, and I know he has spoken untruths so that he can go to the temple. But worse, he laughs about it, and thinks it humorous that folks can be so easily deceived. He even laughed when my sis showed him the letter she had found—laughed and told her that the girl in Utah would be better for his business, better because she was prettier and more outgoing than my sister. Then he walked out on my sister.

"Well, when my sis told us that, I guess I saw red. I told Ma that I was going to Logan to draw rein on Billy's wedding and that nothing was going to stop me. I was going to find me a bishop or somebody and tell them just what sort of dandy Billy really is. They'd stop it sure, then. I know they would. All they'd need to know is what he's really like."

"Only, I just hadn't counted on this storm . . ."

The silence in the warm kitchen was now intense. Duff glanced at Miranda out of the corner of his eye and saw that she was watching him. As if on signal they both then looked at their daughter Maggie, who was again leaning forward, her expression haggard.

"Do . . . do you remember the name on the letter your sister found?" Maggie asked hesitantly of the younger girl.

"I . . . uh . . . no, I don't. My sister told me, but it was kind of a funny name."

"Was it . . . Mags?"

"Maybe, but I just can't remember."

"And your sister's beau's name is Billy?" Maggie pressed.

"Yeah. Well, actually it is William. William Morgan. Some people call him Budge, but that's only a nickname, and since he doesn't like William, my sis always called him Billy."

Jane's voice continued, but no longer was anyone in the room listening. Duff, his eyes riveted on Maggie, saw her turn away and stare silently out of the window into the snowy darkness. Next he looked at his sweetheart of so many years and saw that Andy, too, was watching her daughter, large tears falling down her cheeks as she did so.

Wiping a stray drop of gratitude from his own eye, Duff finally bowed his head. *Heavenly Father,* his mind sang with rejoicing, *how can I thank thee for protecting our precious daughter? I will be eternally grateful—for her sweet purity that thou hast helped Andy and I protect, for revelation concerning her, for the priesthood which has such great power, for honoring my prayer by hedging up the way of this unrighteous union until Maggie and Andy and I could be exposed to the truth . . .*

Duff prayed silently on, pondering as he did so the wondrous miracle that they had all been witness to. Miranda also prayed her thanks as she comforted her heartbroken but still whole youngest daughter. Jane talked herself to sleep right there at the table. Eventually, Duff carried her up to a spare bedroom, after which Miranda put her to bed. Once she was settled, the concerned couple returned to the kitchen. There Maggie, her eyes flashing and her jaw set, was still standing, staring out of the window.

"I'll tell you what," she suddenly said as she turned toward the stairs to her room. "I'm not going to bed until a certain Budge Morgan comes through that door! Then I'll tell him what for! You can bet on that, and take it to the bank."

With determined tread Maggie then ascended the stairs, and Duff and Miranda were left alone to ponder their daughter's words.

"Maggie mustn't be so angry," Miranda said then, sounding worried.

"That's righteous indignation, Andy," Duff responded gently. "And in my opinion, she has every right in the world to feel that way."

"But we're told to turn the other cheek."

Duff smiled. "Oh, she will. You've taught her right, Andy, and in time she'll come to that. But, for now, give her the right to be angry. She's earned it. And believe you me, it'll be good for Brother Budge to hear what she has to say. He's earned it, too. I'm just thankfuller than somewhat that it isn't me she'll be lighting in on."

"And you feel good about that?"

"Feel good?" Duff asked with a wide smile. "Miranda, my dear, I never felt better about anything in my whole life. In my opinion, it'll be sort of like Jesus driving the money changers from the temple. But you're right. I do think we had better start praying again, praying that in time Maggie's heart will be softened toward Budge. That way she can forgive him and get on with her life."

"Exactly," Miranda agreed. "She needs to reach a point where she is sincerely praying that sometime, somehow, Budge Morgan will learn the principle of integrity, and then find someone suitable to accompany him to the holy temple."

Duff Wilkey smiled again and took his wife's hand in his. "You're right, Andy," he said as he pulled her toward him. "Just like always, you're exactly right."

Meanwhile, outside the snug farmhouse kitchen located on Otter Creek, the early fall blizzard continued to rage—

Friday, November 4, 1910

An Arroyo in Southwestern Wyoming

By November 4 the Williams Wave has begun to move more rapidly along the cold front we have been following. The polar jet stream has also completed its shift toward the east-northeast, and the prevailing westerlies push the cold front out of Utah in that direction, the wave remaining beneath the jet stream as it slides along the front.

As it moves eastward, the Williams Wave and its associated cold front continues to whip up high winds and to dump unusually heavy amounts of snow across the high, arid plains of southwest Wyoming.

Wind is actually nothing more than movements of air — cold air falling and warm air rising. The entire United States is dominated by a general wind pattern called the prevailing westerlies, which we have mentioned earlier. Our general wind circulations are the result of the sun's uneven heating of the earth, influenced by the earth's rotation. Air is heated much more intensely at the equator than at the poles. Thus, warm, light air rises in the tropics, while at the same time the cold, heavy air sinks at the poles. The rising tropical air moves northward across the rotating earth before cooling and sinking again at around 30 degrees north latitude. The cold polar air on its trek south from the top of the world meets the sinking air from 30 degrees north latitude and "bulldozes" it skyward again at about 60 degrees north latitude.

Between these two wind circulation cells in the northern hemisphere is a third one which prevails at the midlatitudes. The earth's rotation pulls the winds from all three cells to set up the prevailing wind patterns that we see in the northern hemisphere—the polar easterlies in northern latitudes, the prevailing westerlies in middle latitudes, and the trade winds in southern latitudes.

While winds such as the trade winds are fairly constant, our prevailing westerlies are not, and in fact they shift back and forth with the seasons. These are the winds that create our forever-changing weather conditions. If there were no winds, our weather would always be the same.

Such winds, enhanced by the rapid movement of our cold front and its attached Williams Wave as they throw upward the warmer air masses that get in their way, have an interesting impact on the understanding of three young brothers.

WHERE AND WHEN

"Well, you gonna do it or not?"

Ren Halgeson looked at his two younger brothers, Joe and Bob, thought about what they had been discussing, and finally shrugged his shoulders.

Outside of the sheep wagon the wind was blowing fiercely, and with each gust the little wagon shook and trembled as if it were in an earthquake. Ren thought of that, and once again considered the position he and his brothers were in.

"Before this thing hit us," he asked, "did either of you get a notion of exactly where we are?"

For a moment there was silence in the small wagon, silence broken only by the sound of the wind, the fire in the small cookstove, and the occasional stirring of the two dogs who lay side by side on the narrow floor.

"I think," Joe ventured, "that Black Mountain and the Devil's Playground are off to the south of us a bit—maybe even a little to the southeast."

"I wasn't paying much attention," Bob admitted. "Tip and I were too busy trying to drive that one bunch of sheep into the face of the storm. But if Joe's right, then Soaphole Spring ought to be somewhere nearby."

"It is," Ren agreed thoughtfully. "It's behind us. I thought that was the ridge we passed, but you've confirmed what I was thinking. That makes it about equal distances from here back to Green River or from here down to Lyman. Forty, fifty miles either direction. Too far to ride for it."

"We could try," Bob ventured.

"No, too chancy. Besides, we can't afford to leave the sheep. You both know that this herd is all that Pa has left. Joe, is the entire herd down in this arroyo?"

"Far as I know, Ren. They won't be drifting, either. I think they were real thankful to get out of the teeth of that wind."

"So was I. How about the horses, Bob?"

"I tied Button and Diana in the lee of the wagon here. I think the rest will stay bunched with 'em."

"Good idea. Button's the most wandering sorry fool of a plug to ever come down the pike, and Diana's not much better. For the life of me I can't figure out why Pa ever agreed to the swap that gave him those two critters."

Joe and Bob grinned. Well they knew their father's affection for the two animals in question, and Ren's unswerving animosity toward them. It was almost as if there were a personal war going on, the way Ren yelled at the two horses and the way the two horses acted so contrary toward Ren. Yet for everybody else, the horses did their work well and without complaint. But they were both wanderers.

"So how about it, Ren? You going to do it? What you suggested?"

"I don't know," Ren replied as he shook his head. "How's the wood in the possum belly?"

"Half full, maybe a little more."

"How about the box you're sitting on?"

"She's full. But even with both piles, Ren, we're liable to run out long before morning, I can tell you that."

"Yeah, that's what I was thinking, too. Either of you see any other wood around—besides sage, I mean?"

"There's some willows about a quarter mile down the arroyo," Bob responded.

"Big?"

"Naw, little stuff. It'd be worse than gathering sage."

"Then why'd you even bring it up?" Ren asked disgustedly.

"You asked if there was any other wood around," Bob replied defensively. "You didn't say what kind."

"Why, you chuckleheaded—"

"Ren, Bob," Joe said softly, "this isn't either the time or the place for one of your famous family feuds. If we're going to get through this hummer with Pa's sheep and maybe even our own lives, we'd better be united."

Soberly Ren nodded. "You're right, Joe. I . . . I'm sorry, Bob."

"Me, too," Bob said softly. "I was just trying to get your goat, and I hadn't ought to do that so much."

Ren grinned. "You surely hadn't."

At that instant the sheep wagon was rocked by another icy blast, both dogs whimpered, and all three young brothers looked at each other, no longer even trying to hide their fear.

"That was a bad one," Joe said when the gust had passed.

"Amen. And I've got me a feeling it's going to get worse."

"Brrrr, it's cold," Bob said as he hugged himself. "This sheepskin coat feels like paper, the cold's coming through it so fast. Can't we stoke the stove a little higher?"

"She's stoked to the top," Ren replied. "Much more and she'll be glowing cherry red. The problem, Bob, is the wind. This here canvas-covered wagon wasn't designed to keep out hurricanes, you know. At least we're dry, and the wind isn't hitting us full in the face like it might be."

"I reckon," Joe added, "that we had ought to be thankful for small favors."

"They're better than none at all, that's for certain."

For a few moments the three teenage brothers sat silently, alone with their thoughts and the storm that raged just a thin sheet of canvas away from them. Twice furious blasts of wind rocked the small sheep wagon, and each time the two dogs whimpered their discomfort.

"Darn mutts," Joe finally said. "Maybe we had ought to put them outside. Then they can see what real trouble is like."

"They'd just curl up in a snowbank with their tails over their noses and wait it out," Ren responded with a grin. "It's up here where the world is shaky that they get frightened. Ain't that so, Tippy? Ain't that so?"

While Ren rubbed the dog's ears, Bob pulled one of the blankets from the bunk and wrapped it about himself. Seeing him, Joe reached out and did the same.

"You know, fellers," Ren said as he watched them, "what we had really ought to do is all climb into that bunk together. Then we can all use all the blankets and probably have enough left over that we can give one to the dogs."

"What we had *really* ought to do," Joe said in response, "is to have you do what you talked about doing earlier."

Soberly Ren nodded. "Yeah, I've been thinking on that myself."

"Well," Joe went on, "I'd do it myself, Ren, but I don't hold the Melchizedek Priesthood like you do. You're the only one who's got the power."

"Besides which," Bob added, "you yourself told us that your patriarchal blessing promises you power over all the elements of the earth, this storm happening to be one such element."

"Or two, or three," Joe concluded. "Ren, if ever the elements needed to be controlled, it's now. Just listen to that wind howling out there. It sounds like the banshees that Ella's always reading to us about out of her storybooks. If we don't do something and do it soon, we're going to find ourselves blown over, and then there will be trouble."

Ren nodded. "I know. I keep thinking the same thing. It's just that . . . well, I haven't ever done anything like this before, and I . . . I . . . ."

"You scared, Ren?"

Nineteen-year-old Ren looked at his younger brother. "A little," he finally replied.

"Scared that it won't work?"

"I . . . well, I don't think so," Ren replied quietly. "I'm pretty sure it will work, all right. It's just that, well, I'm not sure I know how to do it, and I don't want to make any mistakes."

"How's easy," Bob declared as if he had had all the experience in the world. "Was it me, I'd do the same thing fellers do when they baptize folks. Just use different words is all."

Ren looked at his youngest brother, new appreciation in his eyes. "I hadn't thought of that," he said slowly, "but I believe you're right, Bob. Now if I can just come up with the words."

"Pa says to let the Holy Ghost put the words in our mouths," Joe stated then. "Maybe if we all pray together, that'll help what you are trying to do."

"Good idea," Ren stated. "Let's all pray. Bob, you start, then you go next, Joe. I'll finish it, and then I'll pray a priesthood blessing."

In that manner the brothers prayed, pouring out their souls to God in three very short, very simple prayers. When they had concluded, Ren stood and faced his two brothers. Then, with trembling voice, he closed his eyes and commanded the storm to cease that very instant.

Opening his eyes, he waited with his two brothers, all of them straining to hear a lessening in the shrill power of the wind. But as the small sheep wagon shook anew with nature's unleashed forces, all were quickly convinced that the storm had only grown worse.

"What went wrong?" Joe asked, finally breaking the silence.

"Maybe Ren got the words mixed up."

"I don't know if I did or not," Ren responded worriedly. "I just did what Pa told me to do if I ever gave a blessing, and just said the words that came into my mind. As far as I know, that storm ought to be stopping."

"Maybe it is, and we just need to exercise our faith."

"Does that howling sound like it's stopping, Joe?" Bob asked almost sarcastically. "Not to me it doesn't. Personally, I think Ren ought to do it again."

"Do it again? You chuckleheaded nincompoop, what will I say this time that I didn't say a few minutes ago?"

"I . . . don't know," Bob replied, sounding stung by his brother's anger.

"Maybe . . . well, maybe we all ought to pray again," Joe said quietly, "and ask to be forgiven of all our sins and shortcomings—like being mean and nasty with each other. If we do that, Ren, then maybe you can do another blessing."

Ren looked at his brother. "Yeah," he said slowly, "that might help. What do you think, Bob?"

Silently Bob nodded his head in agreement.

"Well, I'm sorry, Bob. I didn't mean to be testy."

"Me neither, Ren."

Joe nodded with satisfaction. "That's good. Now, fellers, we've got to do something, and do it quick. Not only is this canvas crate about to blow over on us, but worse, the wind is sucking the heat up out of the stove. I've closed the damper down, but I can hardly feel the blamed fire, and I'm standing right next to the stove."

"Yeah," Ren agreed, "I've seen it do that before, and that's what's happening, all right. At this rate we'll go through our wood in a couple of hours, and not get any good out of it, besides. Uh . . . maybe this time I ought to say the first prayer?"

Again the young men bowed their heads and again sent simple, solemn petitions heavenward. Concluding, Ren once again stood and commanded, according to the promise in his patriarchal blessing, that the elements of the earth be subdued and the storm be stopped.

But again, when Ren had finished, the only thing that either of the three could tell was that the storm most definitely had grown worse.

"This is strange," Ren said as he crowded back close to the stove. "I know I'm not saying anything wrong, but I can't see that much is happening, either."

"Except that this fool wagon is about to blow over!"

"Yeah, except for that. Any other ideas, Robert?"

Slowly the youngest among them shook his head.

"Well, I don't have any either, at least not as far as blessing this storm is concerned. What I do think is that we had all ought to pile in that bunk, get the dogs up there with us, and cover up with everything we've got."

"What about the fire?"

"It's not doing any good, Joe, whether we keep stoking it or not. And frankly, if we can keep warm under all those covers, I'd rather save our wood for when we really need it."

"You don't want to try that blessing thing one last time?"

Ren glanced at his youngest brother. "Not on your life, Bob. This last time I had the feeling like Heavenly Father wasn't any too happy with me. No sir, any more priesthood that's exercised today is going to have to be done by the Lord himself. Me, I'm getting into that bunk."

With these words lingering in the air, the three brothers kicked off their boots and clambered onto the small bunk. There they quickly shed their coats, arranged all the thick blankets with their coats on top of them, adjusted their bodies to each other, and got the two dogs up with them and settled near their feet. Then they lay silently, listening to the fury of the raging storm.

For hours the blizzard pounded against them, shaking the sheep wagon continually as it piled huge drifts of snow in windrows up and down the arroyo. Outside, the horses bunched together, their heads all turned away from the wind. The sheep also bunched, but they did so more randomly, and they refused to move even as snow piled against them and sometimes drifted over them completely.

In the wagon the brothers listened without speaking, and as they grew warm under the thick layer of blankets, one by one they fell asleep. The last to do so, however, was Ren, who finally drifted off with a plea in his mind that Heavenly Father help him to understand why his priesthood blessings had not worked on the fiercely raging storm.

"Hello the wagon!"

Sitting up, Ren blinked the sleepiness out of his eyes. It was daylight, even sunny, it looked like, and his breath hung heavy in the frigid air.

"Joe," he whispered, "you hear anything?"

"Ummph."

"Bob, did you?"

"Say," Robert pleaded, "can't you let a feller sleep?"

"Yeah, I can, but—"

"Hello the camp! Anybody to home?"

In an instant all three brothers were scrambling from the bunk and jerking on their boots.

"Pa," Ren shouted back, "is that you?"

"Nobody else. Thought I sent you three out here to bring in the herd."

Finally pushing the door open against the bank of snow, Ren stepped out into the blinding sunlight, followed one after the other by his two brothers. There they found their father and a couple of other men seated on their horses, looking down on them.

"Burning daylight, boys. Who's in charge of this outfit, anyhow?"

Ren grinned sheepishly. "Pa, we must have slept in a little."

"A little! It's near eight o'clock in the morning. Day's half over already. The horses look good. How's the herd?"

"I . . . I don't know, Pa. Gimme a minute, and I'll go check."

Jim Halgeson laughed. "Don't you worry about it, Ren. The boys and I checked already, and they all look to be doing good. You youngsters did a smart thing holing up in this arroyo. Up on the flat, we'd have probably lost half the herd. Well, what's for chow?"

The three boys looked at each other, grinned, and made a mad scramble for the open door of the sheep wagon. Thirty minutes later a roaring fire in the stove had not only warmed the wagon but had also cooked up a fine, hearty breakfast for all hands.

"That was some blow," Jim Halgeson said a little later as he wiped his plate with a thick slice of bread. "I was some worried about you three."

"How'd you get here so quick, Pa?"

"How'd you think, Bob? We saw the storm coming, got worried, and left yesterday, hoping to meet you. The storm finally forced us into camp last night, not more than two miles from here. Right off this morning we heard the sheep, and that was how we found you so quick. Tell the truth, I was expecting it might take us until tomorrow."

"To my way of thinking," Bob said as he cleaned his own plate, "you were lucky to find us at all. We nearly lost this crazy wagon last night, what with the wind blowing like it was."

Jim Halgeson nodded. "Yeah, I worried about that."

There was silence for a minute, and finally Ren looked at his father. "Pa," he said softly, "something happened last night, something none of us can quite make out. Would you mind if maybe we asked you about it?"

"I take it this is serious," Jim said as he gazed at his eldest son.

"Real serious, sir. And private."

"Boys," Jim Halgeson said as he turned to his two hands, "get everything ready to roll. We'll be out in a few minutes."

With curt nods the two men stepped out of the door, and soon the sounds of horses being saddled and harnessed came through the canvas side of the sheepwagon.

"All right, Ren," Jim said quietly, "tell me what happened."

"It wasn't really what happened that troubles us, Pa. It was what *didn't* happen." Quickly then, and without interruption, Ren went on to describe all that he and his brothers had done with prayer—and with the priesthood—the night before.

"Pa," he finally concluded, "it didn't stop, even a little. Does . . . does that mean that I don't have any priesthood power?"

For a long time Jim Halgeson sat in silence, his eyes on the floor. But then, abruptly, he looked up at his boys. "You all three wondering that same thing?"

Slowly both Joe and Bob nodded.

"Well, boys, don't wonder about it anymore, because it just isn't so. Ren's an elder just like me, and he holds the same priesthood and power as me or the bishop or even the President of the Church, President Joseph F. Smith. But you've got to remember that priesthood can only be used to work righteousness."

"But Pa, what we were doing was righteous. We were just trying to protect us and your herd and wagon from that storm."

"I know that, Joe. But let me ask you a question. Did any of you bother to find out if the Lord wanted this all protected?"

"What do you mean?"

Jim smiled. "Well, maybe he wanted us to lose this stuff."

"Pa, be serious."

"It could be that he did, Bob. Sometimes trials like that are necessary for a feller's growth. But if that wasn't so, then here's another question. Did any of you bother to learn if the Lord wanted the storm stopped, before you tried to do it?"

"Pa, you aren't making sense."

"Why not, Ren? It was the Lord's storm, wasn't it?"

"Well, yeah, I guess it was. But—"

"Boys, listen to me. The priesthood is the Lord's, too, and before anyone can use it with power, they must know that they are using it according to his will and direction. Did any of you do that? Did any of you find out if the Lord had some purposes for that storm that were more important than a few sheep and a wornout sheep wagon?"

Slowly the young men shook their heads.

"Ren," Jim Halgeson went on, "your patriarchal blessing isn't kidding you. Every word in it is gospel truth, if you live worthy of it. The Lord has truly given you power over the elements of the earth, and that power is real. But before he'll let you exercise such a power, he wants you to learn that it is sacred and that it must only be used under his direction. That's part of the law of the priesthood.

"Yes, he heard you last night, and you do have power. But because you needed to learn something, and because you might have been thwarting some higher purposes besides, the Lord apparently chose to overrule you and to let the storm rage on."

"But . . . what could be more important?"

"Any number of things, Robert. Maybe some poor soul out here desperately needed the moisture this snow has in it. Or maybe something bad was prevented from happening because of it, or something good was brought to pass."

"Like teaching me a lesson," Ren said softly.

"Exactly, Ren. Whatever, it is important to remember that despite the fact that we have been ordained to the priesthood, that magnificent power is only on loan and is only to be used under God's direction. Understand now?"

The three young men nodded together.

"Good. There's one other thing I want you to think about. The wagon didn't blow over last night, the sheep didn't drift, and apparently the three of you slept almighty comfortably. Seems to me you couldn't have asked for a better answer to a priesthood prayer than that.

"Now, you boys ready to ride?"

They were, and fifteen minutes later the only evidence that three righteous but still growing young brothers had spent the night in the snow-filled arroyo was churned snow from hundreds of hooves, both large and small—that and a set of tracks made by a sheep wagon's iron tires as it lined out through the new snow for home.

But east of there, the storm raged on.

Saturday and Sunday,
November 5 and 6, 1910

The Wind River Mountains

Again the drama of a cold front being pushed up the side of a mountain range is repeated. The Wind River Range offers strong resistance, and a great deal of precipitation falls on the windward side of the mountains before the cold front moves on. The Williams Wave adds to this, especially on the mountain range's southern end and out into the Great Divide Basin. For the small communities lying in the rough triangle between Rock Springs, Rawlins, and South Pass, Wyoming, it will take several days to dig out of the almost three feet of wind-packed snow they have so quickly received.

But the front is moving quite rapidly now, and the blizzards of Saturday are replaced early Sunday morning with calm winds and widely scattered, gently falling snow.

For an avid young hunter, it is the perfect situation for a successful campaign into the Wind River Mountains above his home—

THE TEACHER

The afternoon air was still, heavy with the scent of pines and aspen, and seventeen-year-old Elijah Altman sensed that he was not alone. Quietly he sat on his horse, his rifle cradled in his arm, while he stared through the sentinel pines at the snow-covered open meadow ahead.

A lone raven called from somewhere far off, but aside from that nothing moved, nothing stirred. It was so still that Elijah could hear the whispering sound made by the softly falling remnants of the snowstorm, a sound that he had never heard before in his entire youthful life.

Without moving Elijah waited, his senses testing what they could, his entire soul alive with the certainty that something unusual was in progress, or perhaps had already happened, in this very place.

Looking quickly elsewhere, he cast his eyes down off the mountain, looking south and west. He was in the Wind Rivers, on the southwest slope of Fremont Peak, Wyoming, though he wasn't exactly certain where. Below him, through miles of snow-shrouded timber, he could make out Titcomb Lake, and farther off still, Island Lake, Lost Lake, and Seneca Lake. It was an incredible country, a lovely country, and he would have been enjoying every minute of this hunt if it hadn't been for the storm—that and the feeling that he wasn't alone.

Maybe this was how the old mountain men had felt when they had been in danger. It couldn't have been much different than this when they and the other early explorers—men such as Jed Smith, Jim Bridger, John C. Fremont, Captain Bonneville, and others—had first found their way through this country.

How Elijah would have loved to have been one of them, free to come and go as he wished, free to see things no man had ever seen before! Surely they, too, had felt the tingle of joy when gazing upon a pristine, snow-covered meadow with nary a track on it by either man or beast. Surely they had felt the sense of not being alone when Indians had been near, the same uneasy sense that young Elijah was feeling now as he stared ahead, trying to locate what was troubling him.

Quietly dismounting, he wrapped one of the horse's reins around a tree limb, patted the horse gently on the neck, and took a few steps forward, his entire being alive to the feeling that he was sharing this time, this place, with another.

For a moment he thought he heard the soft sighing of wind, but raising his eyes he saw no movement in the lodgepoles. Even the single aspen he could see ahead was curiously still. Yet the sighing was still there—faint, distant, almost inaudible—and for a breath or two, he wondered.

Cautiously Elijah stepped forward again, the hammer on his rifle cocked and ready, his keen eyes alert for any movement, any movement at all. Behind him he heard his horse stamping nervously as it shook its head and blew. Old Paint was feeling it, too, this eerie sense of being on the mountain with someone else. Now, if he could only determine what or who it was . . .

Elijah had left home back on Willow Creek long before daylight to secure a little badly needed venison for his family. Of course he had done so over his parents' strenuous objections, but what was new about that? Elijah smiled at the thought, though not happily. It seemed that lately, no matter what he wanted to do, his folks figured him to be wrong—as if he were turning wicked or something. But what utter nonsense that was!

Elijah Altman, wicked? Again he smiled ruefully. He couldn't ever be wicked. He believed in God, kept most of the basic commandments, and sometimes even prayed. He just didn't believe in approaching religion in the same serious, fanatical way that his parents seemed to think was necessary.

Instead, it felt to him that life should be enjoyed, filled with laughter and a continual round of good practical jokes between friends. And such jokes he truly delighted in pulling off at every opportunity. Besides, never were his jokes serious, intended to hurt; rather they were done for the sheer joy of having fun. There were burrs under saddle blankets, pails of water placed over doors, a fresh cow pie on the bishop's front step, and so forth. Elijah just wanted to laugh and to have a good time with his friends. So he pulled all the practical jokes that he could, laughed constantly, and appreciated it immensely when someone else managed to pull a good ol' zinger on him.

But his folks couldn't see things that way. They said he was becoming wicked, and they had their scriptures to prove it. For instance, the deal today was breaking the Sabbath. Of course the family needed meat pretty badly and could ill afford to butcher one of their few beef. And since he was so blasted busy working for his father most every other day, Elijah had decided to go out today, Sunday, to get a deer or maybe even an elk, thus helping to fill the family larder.

But the way his folks had reacted, a body would have thought he had announced that he intended to commit murder. His mother had grabbed the Bible, his father the Doctrine and Covenants, and for nigh onto an hour they had preached at him about keeping the commandments.

Well, Elijah thought as he set his jaw and looked about the still, white meadow, he was entitled to his own views on that subject, and he would follow those views. Nor did his views make him evil, any more than trying to help his family by hunting on Sunday was making him evil. All he wanted out of life was to help his loved ones and to have fun doing so.

But to listen to his parents tell it, he was going straight to hell in a handbasket, with the devil having greased the skids. Of course they wanted to stop what they called his downward course, so they were constantly throwing their beloved scriptures at him, trying to make him see how important it was to keep the commandments.

But by jings, he was tired of hearing about the scriptures! He had even stopped reading them, he was so sick of having their doctrines thrown at him.

Of course, he quickly told himself, that didn't mean that he had stopped loving his family, for he hadn't. Indeed, despite the fact that his parents were now quite elderly, he loved them with all his heart. They were wonderful people, always doing for others, and never selfish. They both worked hard; sometimes too hard, Elijah thought. And they had great faith, too. He had seen literal miracles wrought in the family through the faith of his parents, miracles that could be explained in no other way. Faith and miracles were things the young man didn't altogether understand, though he did believe in them.

For instance, they always called him their miracle son, and he couldn't see any way around admitting it to be true. Why, by the time he had been born, his sister next to him had been eighteen, and his oldest brother, thirty-two. Even more astounding, his mother had been forty-eight, and his father fifty-three. Yet along he had come, surprising the entire world except his parents, who soberly declared that he had been promised to them by the Lord in a blessing given to his mother. Thus Elijah had always been his folks' miracle son.

There were other miracles, too, but the one miracle his folks hadn't been able to pull off, but which brought a smile to Elijah's face whenever he thought of it, was the miracle that would turn him back to studying the scriptures and would stop him from chasing around pulling pranks, enjoying Sundays his way. Elijah knew that sort of miracle didn't even need to happen, but he did enjoy listening to his folks pray for him concerning it. At least he knew that they were thinking of him.

Again moving forward, Elijah scanned the trees, looking for movement. He himself was well concealed, just as he imagined the old mountain men had concealed themselves as they had examined the country they were passing through.

Oh, if he could only have lived back when men were men, when life was free and easy, when he wouldn't have had to be troubled by such serious religious ideas as his folks were trying to force upon him. Why, even if he could have just been a Mormon pioneer, like his mother's folks had been, he would have been satisfied. Of course he didn't know much about them, having never met his grandfather. But in him was a vague memory of his mother's mother, who had died when he was five, and of tales of adventure she apparently told concerning her long-dead husband.

Cautiously Elijah slipped forward to the shelter of another tree, his rifle ready. All morning he had hunted, certain that he would be successful early. Yet he had not seen a living creature, and desperate for success he had ridden farther and farther, at last climbing the mountain that had reached skyward, dominating his horizon as with a beckoning finger ever since his folks had settled on their ranch.

Fremont Peak. Wouldn't it have been something to have been able to name an entire mountain after himself, like old Fremont had done? The Altman range. Now, that had a ring to it. Or Lake Altman, or even the Elijah Altman Hills, by jings. He wouldn't have been choosy. Yes siree, those old boys knew how to live. More than that, they knew what was important in life, and they lived their lives to the fullest.

Well, even if he couldn't be a mountain man or a pioneer, he was going to enjoy life in the same way. His folks were just going to have to accept the fact that their beliefs were just too steep for him. A man could live a good, productive, fun-filled, and adventuresome life without them, and that was exactly what Elijah Altman intended to do!

Again he moved forward, and now the meadow came more clearly into view. Pausing once more, he gazed across it, his breath taken with the incredible beauty of the place. His mind reeling, he walked forward with a measured pace and shortly found himself in the center of the opening in the trees.

He breathed deeply, looked around carefully, and listened intently to the strange sighing. He was feeling the beauty of this meadow with all his heart, and yet he knew even as he attempted to become one with it that no matter how much he tried to see and hear and feel what the meadow had to tell him, he could not possibly comprehend the full wonder of this one spot of mountain. That was because he had not been here first.

Oh, if only he could know who had! How he would have liked to meet that man, sit at his feet and learn from him, see what he had seen, and feel the joy and freedom he must have felt when he first moved across this pristine meadow!

Still, being here this day wasn't all bad! No siree, it wasn't. In fact, somehow the place seemed familiar to him, and as he looked around, Elijah had the feeling that maybe . . .

And then the tingles came again, and Elijah Altman knew once more that another man was there with him, there in that very place on the mountain. He didn't know how he knew, but he knew, and that was certain.

Taking a deep breath to slow his hammering heart, Elijah suddenly wished for his father—his father, who had left all he had in the old country so that he might come to this new land and rest in the cradle of his new religion. There had been many sacrifices as he had settled first in Brigham City, then in Cache Valley, and finally here in Wyoming. But the old man had never regretted his difficulties. Mormonism, he had told Elijah over and over, was the Lord's way of stretching mankind, preparing them for the second coming of the Lord, and he was thankful that he could participate in that preparation.

Elijah had never doubted his father's testimony, or his mother's either. But he did wonder why it always seemed that righteousness was synonymous with seriousness, with being made to toe the line with so many blasted rules and commandments. To him that made no sense, no sense at all.

Yet his father was a good man, one who seemed to know what to do in any sort of emergency. Now, tingling the way he was, it would have been nice to have his father standing behind him.

Nearby the ground rose and then dropped away, and suddenly the young hunter felt that he had to see beyond that rise. Carefully and quietly he climbed, only to find that once he topped the rise, the earth fell quickly away and a small stream appeared below, spread out in a huge and ancient beaver pond.

The unusual sighing was louder now, and Elijah finally recognized it as the murmur of hundreds of tiny tricklets of water cascading down over the old beaver dam. But the old dam was still holding, the water was not frozen, and, judging from the number of freshly chewed aspen trunks around him, Elijah knew that the lodge out in the pond was still occupied.

Now all but the water was bathed in white, and truly Elijah had never seen anything of such surpassing beauty. He breathed a sigh of wonder and relief, smiled, and then watched with surprised interest as a beaver suddenly surfaced and swam to the far bank. The beaver's wake spread out in a widening V behind it, and suddenly Elijah recognized the sign.

The beaver was pointing the way, and he, Elijah Altman, had but to go in the direction of that arrow to find the other man, or whatever else it might be, whose presence he had been feeling for the past several moments.

Back on Old Paint, the young man rode across the meadow, down the steep slope, and through the stream where it ran shallow below the dam. On the other side he kicked his mount up the far hill and had not ridden more than fifty yards when he saw it—a small cave up under some overhanging boulders.

Pulling rein, Elijah studied that hole. Under normal conditions, he knew he would never have seen it. The hole was black, but so was the rock it lay in, making the cave all but invisible. But the fresh snow had made the difference, and now he sat gazing at it, wondering what he should do.

"Heavenly Father," he finally said, "if you happen to be

listening, my folks would want me to pray in a situation like this, and maybe this time they'd be right. I've been feeling all spooky for the last little while, like somebody's watching me. I'm probably all alone and going a little nuts, but just in case, I'd appreciate a little help here."

Carefully Elijah looked all around the small cave opening, but so far as he could tell there had been no disturbance in the snow leading up to it. That was good. But then, by jings, what was it he was feeling? He was skittish as a spring colt, and he could hardly keep from kicking Old Paint a good one and getting the two of them down out of there.

But on the other hand, he felt certain that there was something in that cave, something that he had been led to, something he had to see.

Sliding out of the saddle, Elijah once again wrapped a rein around a nearby tree limb. Then, his rifle cocked and ready, he climbed closer to the hole in the rocks.

"Say!" he shouted finally when he was all set. "You in the cave! Come on out of there!"

The snow muffled any echo his voice might have caused, but Elijah waited in vain for any other response to his order. The entire mountain was still, utterly silent, save for the barely audible whisper of falling snow.

By jings but he was spooked! There was something in that cave, maybe *somebody*, and he knew it just as certainly as he knew he was standing in the snow worrying about it. The hair on his neck was crawling, and he was shaking uncontrollably despite the fact that he was not in the least bit cold.

Reaching down, Elijah scooped up some snow and quickly fashioned a snowball. With accuracy born of long years of schoolyard practice he let it fly and then watched with satisfaction as the round missile sailed into the hole. Expectantly he waited, his rifle ready. But nothing came out— no sound, no protest, nothing.

Suppose, he thought then, that he had been a mountain man. Suppose he had been Dick Wootton or Broken-Hand Fitzpatrick or Hugh Glass, and there was a bear or maybe even an Indian holed up in there. That being the case, what would one of them have done?

When put in that light, the answer was patently simple— they'd go in after them, and do it sudden. Those men had been afraid of nothing, and they hadn't let such things as haunts buffalo them either.

Stepping back, Elijah worked his way under a large pine. There he found a branch that was not only dry but also heavy with pitch. This he hacked off the tree.

Going back to Old Paint, he took some sulphur matches from the saddlebags, cupped his hand, and the second match brought the pitchy branch to flame. Armed with that in one hand and his rifle in the other, Elijah moved slowly back up the rocks to the mouth of the cave. Then, stooping down, he scrambled through the low opening and was inside.

Looking around, letting his eyes adjust, he realized for the first time that the floor of the cave lifted sharply just a few feet back from the opening. The ceiling also lifted, though less steeply, and he could see that he would have to make a crawling climb if he went much further. Yet feeling drawn to continue, even compelled, he scrambled to the rise, dropped to his knees, and worked his way up the steep, slick incline.

For maybe a dozen feet he climbed, having a hard go of it, and then the floor leveled off and Elijah found himself in a small, roomlike opening. The floor was thick with dry dust, and by the light of the torch he could see that no animals had been in this hole to leave their tracks, at least not in very recent times.

Lifting the torch higher, Elijah found that he could stand, and he had just done so and had taken his first deep breath to calm his pounding heart when the light of the torch revealed the other man.

Gasping and stepping back with surprise, young Elijah nearly fell back down the steep incline. But quick reflexes saved him, he regained his balance, and then he stared with wonder at the cave's other occupant—a moldering skeleton that lay almost hidden by a small pile of rocks.

"How . . . how long have you been here, old timer?" Elijah whispered, at a loss for what else to say or do.

The sound of his own voice was somehow reassuring, and so cautiously Elijah stepped forward, his torch held high so that he might better see. And right away he felt the hairs on the nape of his neck lifting again.

This man had been a white man, of that Elijah was certain. He had been white, and he had also been murdered!

Stepping around the hardened leather boots that still contained the bones of the man's feet, the young hunter carefully lifted the rotting arrow from the man's chest cavity. And even more carefully, he examined it.

"You were killed by Indians!" he exclaimed with wonder. "By jings! Just how long have you been here, old man?"

Again Elijah looked at the iron-tipped arrow, turning it in his hands, wondering what warrior had made and then fired it, wondering what tribe the Indian had come from. Finally setting the frail arrow aside, he carefully examined the ancient but hardly rusted rifle, knife, and weathered powderhorn that lay among the bones. And as he did so, he wondered that the Indian had not taken such treasured weaponry at the time he had killed the man.

"Wait a minute," he said with realization as he held the powderhorn in his hands. "You weren't killed here in this cave at all, were you, old timer? You got yourself wounded, and then you crawled in here to hole up until you got better— only for some reason you just didn't make it. By jings, if this isn't something! A real, honest-to-goodness mountain man!"

His heart racing, Elijah Altman stood and stared down at the skeletal remains. So this had been a mountain man, one of that breed of men who had known the world as it really was, had faced it squarely, and had without complaint taken what it had offered, laughing heartily, and had then given equally in return.

What this hero must have seen! Elijah's imagination raced. What adventures he must have lived! What freedom he must have enjoyed! No fetters to bind him, no folks to worry and fret over what he might be doing on the Sabbath, no scriptures to be pounded into his ears, no commandments to worry about.

In the flickering light of the cave, Elijah suddenly spotted a corner of something protruding from beneath a rock near the bones of the man's hand. Reaching down, he carefully removed the rock and was amazed to discover a folded scrap of paper, yellowed but not brittle.

Carefully opening it, Elijah discovered that the writing —in a clear, neat hand—was still legible. Shaking a little with excitement as he adjusted his flickering torch, the young hunter began to read:

Oct 1854

Ifn you red this you arnt Indan. Good. Blakfot got me, and I run, but not fur enuf. Now my hoss is gone and I cant get the arrer out so Im kilt. Tell Rachl Im sory. Shot 2 good elk in the medo yondr but them braves

mustv wantd em worsn me. Same with my hosses. Hop
Rachl and the litl ones don't starv this wintr on accnt of
tht. Got my tresur hiddn undr the rocks bhint me. Id be
bholdn if its got to Rachl and the litl ones. Theyl be
with the Mormons—jst ask whar from Bro Brighm. Tel
Rachl shes a good womn—durn good. The Lords work
is tru, and be sur to have her tel the litl ones I knowd it
and died firm in the faith. Dont frget to giv em my tresur.

Thanks, Elijah Ne——

Dumbfounded, young Elijah Altman read the note again
and again. It was spooky, reading it. Fact is, it was almost as
if the old timer was sitting there talking to him, telling him
what had happened up in the meadow he had just crossed.
Even more spooky was the fact that the man had been named
Elijah. Now that was enough to give a feller the fluttering fan-
tods!

And imagine, the old geezer with the arrow in his chest
had been a *Mormon*. Somehow Elijah had never pictured
men of this breed—mountain men and hunters—as being
members of the Church. But this man had sure enough been
Mormon. Despite the fact that he had been a hunter and had
been alone in this wild land in a wild time, had even fought
some wild Indians and lost, he was still a Latter-day Saint.

Shaking his head with continual wonder, Elijah read the
note again. Yes, the word was still there, the word he hadn't
dared let himself think about the first few times through. But
it was still there, so this time he let his mind dwell on it.

Treasure. Each time he read the note, the word *treasure*
sort of jumped out at young Elijah Altman. But for some
reason he was afraid to look where the dead man had directed. Maybe, he thought, there would be nothing there.
Maybe someone had already found it and had removed it
from the cave. But no, that didn't make sense. Somebody else
would surely have taken the arrow, the old rifle, and the other
foofaraw when they got the treasure. So that meant that the
old timer's wealth pretty much had to be where he had hidden it.

Bending over, Elijah placed the letter and his rifle down,
then propped the burning pine torch between some boulders.
Next, moving carefully, he began laying aside the stones that
were piled behind the man's crumpled remains.

At first he found nothing, and he felt the bitter feeling of disappointment at being too late. In his mind he had been conjuring up visions of wealth—gold or maybe silver, raw or minted, it didn't seem to matter. What mattered was that it would be his, and at a youthful age he would become a wealthy man.

Of course there was the matter of the dead man's family, Elijah thought guiltily, and of his plea that the treasure be returned to them. But young Elijah was already working his way through that little problem, too, and he knew that, given time, he would feel good about his decision to keep the money for himself. After all, the man's last name was written illegibly, so Elijah couldn't possibly trace the family. But even if he could, the woman, Rachel Ne-whatever-it-was, would be long dead by now, as might all or at least most of the little ones the mountain man had spoken of. And even if they weren't dead, it was anybody's guess who or where they might now be. Therefore, the young hunter reasoned, he need feel no pressure to locate them, or even to instigate a search. By all rights the treasure should be his, would be his. But still he was feeling strangely guilty.

Suddenly his fingers found an object that, while hard, did not feel quite like the surrounding rocks. Carefully Elijah worked it loose and lifted it, and in the flickering light he realized that he held in his hand a time-hardened, securely fastened leather pouch, complete with neck strap.

"By jings," he said aloud as he turned the pouch back and forth. "What do you know? A possibles bag. Probably holds his shot and wadding, though it doesn't feel very heavy. Maybe he used it all up fighting those Indians."

The pouch seeming too small to hold real treasure, Elijah placed it on the floor by his rifle, and then he tore at the rocks again, this time more indiscriminately, scattering them throughout the room. But ten minutes later, with the flame nearly burned out on his makeshift torch, the young man had to face the fact that if there was any treasure in that room at all it would have to be in the possibles pouch at his feet.

Hurriedly then, before he lost his flickering light, young Elijah gathered the man's antiquated gear, as well as the fatal arrow, and carried them down to the cave opening. Going back, he took up his own rifle and the small black pouch, and then he looked for a last time upon the remains of Elijah Ne——.

"Mister . . . I mean Brother Whoever-you-are," he said softly as he took off his hat, "I'm sorry I can't do better for you today. Maybe I can come back some other time and see that you get a marker and a decent burial. I'll also see that your rifle and other gear are well cared for. As for your treasure, well, don't you worry none about it. I . . . uh . . . well, I don't reckon it'd do me much good to try chasing down any of your next-of-kin. Likely they're long dead by now, anyway."

Elijah paused, still wondering at his guilt. For some reason it was a terrible thing, truly weighing down on him. Maybe if he made the old man a promise of some sort . . .

"Uh," he finally muttered, "you have my word of honor, sir, that I will cherish that treasure of yours, and use it in the best way I possibly can — not frivolous like my folks say I usually am. For a fact, I'll do my best to build something with it, just like you would have done, had you made it past that one last arrow. Amen."

His guilt somewhat assuaged by the spur-of-the-moment promise, Elijah replaced his hat and carried his rifle and the pouch down to where he had stacked the rest of the dead man's gear. There, sitting in the mouth of the cave, he once again examined the old leather possibles bag.

Unlatching the strap that held it closed, Elijah carefully pulled back the flap and looked inside. There was no shot or wadding, but he did find an oilcloth packet, which he also carefully opened. In it were some papers, yellowed with age, but also not brittle, and another small, well-wrapped packet.

Feeling a little like an intruder, young Elijah looked quickly through the papers, discovering that they were letters addressed to the man in the cave. Two had been signed by the man's wife, Rachel, and the third by a person called Francine. And all were dated, incredibly, in the early 1850s.

His heart pounding, Elijah then looked at the remaining packet. If there was treasure, this had to be it. But what could be so valuable, he wondered as he turned it this way and that in the afternoon light, and yet be so small? He couldn't guess, but taking a deep breath, he began unwrapping the oilcloth that had been so carefully secured by the Mormon mountain man.

Down off the rocks his horse nickered, somewhere down the mountain a raven called, and it finally stopped snowing — Elijah noticed none of them. With trembling fingers he peeled back the oilcloth, pulled it away, and looked with total shock upon the dead mountain man's most precious mortal treasure—a book.

Slowly then he turned the book over so he could read the title, and then Elijah Altman didn't know whether he wanted to laugh or cry. In his hands, the young practical joker and scorner of serious religion held a leather-bound copy of—the Book of Mormon.

For a moment Elijah simply stared at it, his mind all awhirl. Then, moving almost woodenly, he opened the cover, and there he discovered the dead man's full name, neatly printed—*Elijah Newling.*

Much later, seated on Old Paint, Elijah Altman paused where he could see off down Fremont Peak toward his home. Far below him the snow-covered Wyoming plains stretched away south and west, toward the blue horizon. For some time he just looked, devouring the beauty, and thinking of all that had transpired in his life.

He knew as he sat there that the presence he had felt on the mountain that day had been the spirit of the mountain man, Elijah Newling. He knew, too, that old Elijah had wanted him to find his remains, and his treasure, as well. And he knew finally, but with the greatest certainty of all, that it had been the faith and prayers of his folks that had brought it all to pass.

With a wide smile, the young hunter removed his hat and looked skyward. "Well, Heavenly Father," he said amiably, "you tricked me! You fooled me good, and my hat's off to you for the fine way you did it. I ain't been snookered like that in a long time."

Down the mountain the crow called again, and Elijah's smile grew wider still. "Yes sir, you got me to attend a meeting, whether I wanted to go to church or not, and that's some better than my folks have been able to do. Worse, you got me to take an oath that I'd cherish that old man's scriptures and use them like he did. Whewee, Heavenly Father! I hope you know that's a real coup you counted on that one, feeling as I have about the scriptures.

"But I took the oath, of my own free will I swore it, and now you'll find I'm a man of my word. Starting now, Heavenly Father, I'll cherish that Book of Mormon and study it just like, well, just like Grandpa Newling did before that arrow took his life."

Shaking his head, Elijah thought about that—about the fact that he had come all this way, wandering all over creation, so to speak, and all the while being unknowingly led directly to the lost remains of his own grandfather, Elijah Newling.

And young Elijah knew he was right about that, too. His grandmother had been named Rachel Newling, and, by jings, his own mother's name was Francine!

But the final clincher, the one that really did it for him, was his mother's well-worn question, often asked rhetorically, that he had been named after his righteous grandfather and so why the dickens didn't he act a little more like him?

"Yes sir, Lord," Elijah Altman declared, smiling again, "that's the grandest joke I've ever seen, and I'll be abiding by it. But one thing. If it's all the same with you, Heavenly Father, I'd like to keep smiling and having fun whilst I'm about all this religious stuff I promised Grandfather Newling that I'd do. I figure if you and he can pull such a stunt as this on me, then I had ought to be able to pull a few more innocent little zingers on some of the folks down below.

"If it's all the same to you, I'll be getting right after it, too, before I get too old to enjoy such tomfoolery."

Still smiling, young Elijah Altman then replaced his hat, and just as suddenly removed it and looked upward again.

"Name of Jesus," he added quickly, "amen."

And then, his smile still wide, he headed Old Paint down the snow-covered slope. For him, the storm had passed and he was on his way home, in more ways than one. But further east, moisture continued to fall—

Monday, November 7, 1910

Cheyenne, Wyoming

Immediately behind the front we have been following, temperatures take an immediate drop due to the coldness of the air mass following the front. Then, as a high-pressure system—a dome of air—slides in to take the cold front's place, temperatures begin a gradual climb and clear skies allow the sun to begin melting the snows so recently deposited.

Considerably weakened by the time it reaches the eastern border of Wyoming, our cold front drifts in a northeasterly direction out over the Great Plains. Its fury spent as it slammed across the Rocky Mountains, the front now exhibits little stormy energy as it "wimps" toward Canada. It may develop into a major system over Nova Scotia or out over the Atlantic, but most of those who felt its fury have already forgotten it.

One, though, who has not forgotten, sits worriedly in his home on the outskirts of Cheyenne, Wyoming—

TRUSTING

"There is something wrong, Sheriff. I . . . I thought you ought to know."

Samuel Chavez looked up at the most famous midwife in all of the area north of Cheyenne. In her face he could see concern, but more than that he could see fear, and Sam Chavez was a man who had learned, wearing his tin star for as long as he had worn it, to read fear.

"What do you mean, Abby?" He asked slowly, and very calmly, doing what he could to diffuse her fright. After all, his five children were seated around the room with him, and it wouldn't help a whole lot for he or Abby to get the bunch of them all riled up.

Abigale Wagner shook her head. "I hardly know what I mean. Em's way bigger than she ought to be, though I'm positive that she's only carrying one baby. But there's something else."

"Abby," Sam said as he rose slowly to his feet, "let me take you outside onto the porch. Maybe a breath of fresh air will help."

Dutifully Abby followed Sam out of the door and onto the porch, from which the white world of still-drifting snow could be seen, felt, and heard. There she pulled her sweater more tightly around her, and Sam turned his back to the constant wind.

"All right, Abby," he said as he looked her in the eye, "what's wrong with my wife?"

"I . . . wish I knew," Abby replied as quick tears sprang to her eyes. "I can hear and feel the baby, but not like I could a short while ago. For some reason that baby is growing weaker, and Emily isn't ready to deliver."

"So it's the baby you're worrying about?"

Abby shook her head. "Not altogether. Emily's in pain, Sam. Real pain. I've never seen anything like this in my life, but something's gone wrong inside her body that is causing her to spasm with pain, even if I don't do one single thing other than to simply touch her. I . . . well, I don't know what to do."

"Doc Steele only lives half a mile from here, Abby. Should I send one of the boys to fetch him?"

Silently the woman nodded.

"Anything else?"

Abby sighed. "I wish she could be in a hospital, Sam."

"That's all the way down on the other side of Cheyenne, Abby. Roads are drifted over, telephone lines are down. There just isn't any way on this earth that we could get Em down to that hospital in time to do any good."

Slowly the midwife nodded her head. "I know. It's just that, well, there's a Doctor Feldstone there who specializes in these sorts of problems. Doc Steele is a fine man, Sheriff, but whatever's wrong with Emily, I have a feeling that it'll be bigger than either he or I can deal with."

Sam nodded silently and ducked his head as another frigid blast whipped around the corner of his old frame house, driving snow through the screens of the porch.

"Can you detect anything being wrong with the baby?" he asked then.

"Not a thing. It has presented itself perfectly, and if Emily was dilated a little more, we could go ahead and have a birth."

"So the problem really is Emily."

Abby nodded.

Sam took a deep breath. "Send Jacob out here, will you, Abby? Then you do what you can."

The woman disappeared through the door, and Sam stood still, staring into the white of what was now mostly a ground blizzard.

"Heavenly Father," he breathed as sudden tears started at his eyes, "please, no. Don't take Emily now, or the baby, either one. How can I raise those little children in there without her? Or this new baby? I haven't ever asked for much, being raised by my mother to be thankful for what you had already done. But now, dear God, with all my heart and soul I am asking—please make it so things aren't so bad with my Emily."

"You want me, Pa?" Jacob asked as he came through the door.

Sam looked down at his eight-year-old son, a boy who in all things tried so hard to be a man. How lucky he and Em were to have children such as little Jacob and the others!

"Yes, Jake, I need you. Can you get to Doc Steele's house in this blizzard?"

Soberly the boy nodded. "I can on Skippy, Dad. She's steady, and we'll just follow the fences."

"Good. Then go get him, son, but don't take time to saddle up. Just hurry as fast as you can."

"Is it Mom?"

Sam nodded silently.

"Is she . . ."

"Jake, it looks real bad, and I'm not going to kid you about it. I don't even know if Doc Steele can help, but I'm hoping. Pray all you can, son, like the rest of us will be doing. And hurry!"

Without another word Jake spun back into the house, and hardly more than a minute later Sam heard the back door slam shut behind the hurrying boy. Smiling with a feeling of love and pride, he then went back into the house.

"Sam."

At the sound of his wife's weakened voice, Sam entered the kitchen, where he had moved her bed in preparation for the baby's birth.

"I'm here, Em," he said as he gently placed his hand on hers.

"Help me, Sam," she pleaded as she gripped his fingers. "Everything's dark, and I feel so awful cold. What's going wrong?"

"I don't know, honey. Abby says the baby looks just fine."

"But it isn't kicking anymore, Sam! Something's awful wrong, and I . . . I'm scared."

"Now Em, there's no need to be frightened."

"Don't you go playing sheriff on me, Samuel Chavez!" Emily suddenly declared with great force. "I'm not a crowd you have to control, or some sorry fool you have to arrest, either one. I'm your wife, darn it, and I think I deserve a little honesty."

Grinning, Sam looked up at the surprised Abby and winked. "Now you see why I married her?" he asked.

Abby nodded vigorously, and Sam turned once again to his wife. "Em, I don't know what to tell you. Abby thinks, like you, that something may have gone wrong—serious wrong. Jake's gone for Doc Steele, but until he gets here, I really don't know what else to say."

"Am . . . am I going to die?"

"I hope not, Em."

"I . . . hope not, too. We've still got so much to enjoy together."

"We've always been broke, Em, and you've had to work way too hard."

"No harder than you, Sam. Besides, that's what folks do who love each other as we do."

"Yeah, I suppose you're right."

"And look at the children, Sam. No one on this earth has better children than we do! Or handsomer ones, either. And I'll bet this little one will be the cream on the top of the milk pail. Oh, why . . . why can't I just have this baby?"

"You aren't ready, Emily," Abby responded from the other side of the room. "I'd push and help things along, but you can't stand to have me touch you."

"Too much pain," Emily said weakly. "None of the other children felt like this."

She grew silent, and so too did Sam and Abby, neither of them knowing what to do or say.

"Sam."

"I'm here, Em."

"If . . . if I die, promise me you'll marry again, Sam. Real fast!"

"Now Emily—"

"I mean it! You'll do no good alone, and neither will the children. Laura Hinckle would be a good choice, Sam. She's alone, too, and she has always loved the children . . ."

Emily's voice drifted off, and Sam remained silent beside her, his mind churning with questions. Was she going to die? Was his beloved Emily going to give her life while giving birth to another? Was he truly going to be alone?

For a moment he thought of Widow Hinckle, wondering— but no, that was crazy! Emily would make it, and she needed all his faith and concentration. This was certainly not the time to start thinking about another wife!

But what if Emily didn't make it? Sam had faced death quite regularly in his duties as sheriff, and he had always managed to handle it unemotionally. But, well, this was altogether different, and he knew, as his throat constricted with emotion, that he was no better prepared for such an eventuality than any of the others he had worked with during his term as sheriff. Why, if his beloved Emily left him, what would he do? How could he manage to go on alone?

"Sam," Emily suddenly asked, "can . . . can I have a blessing?"

"I gave you one already, honey."

"I . . . I know. But I want another one."

"As soon as Doc Steele gets here, we'll anoint you and give you a proper one. I promise."

"Is he . . . almost here?"

Sam looked at the floor. "I think so, Em. Now here, let me rub your shoulders."

Sam started to do that, touching his wife's shoulder near her neck, and Emily screamed while her entire body went into spasms of pain. Jerking his hand back, Sam stared helplessly while his beloved companion writhed and twisted on the bed, her breath coming in short, ragged sobs.

Finally unable to bear watching his wife any longer, Sam turned away.

"Honey . . ." Emily said weakly as the spasms slowly subsided, "you need to be . . . with the children . . . I'll be fine . . ."

Nodding and wiping his eyes, Sam went slowly back into the parlor, where his children were staring wide-eyed at the doorway. "Kids," he said gently, "things . . . well, they aren't going too well in there."

"Is that why you sent Jacob for Doctor Steele?"

"Yes, Mary. That's why."

"Is it the baby, Dad?"

The questioner this time was seven-year-old Adam, a bright lad who had no fear of anything alive.

"Partly, Adam. The baby isn't doing so well. But neither is your mother."

"Daddy . . ."

Sam turned and met the rush of his eldest child and daughter, nine-year-old Sarah, who threw her arms around him and commenced sobbing.

"Please don't let her die, Daddy. Please don't."

"We're doing all we can do, Sarah. But I think this is in Heavenly Father's hands."

"Can we . . . ask him, then?"

Sam nodded. "I think we should do just that. Sarah, you pray first. Then Mary, you can pray second, Adam will be third, and Nick, will you say a prayer for Mommy?"

The three-year-old boy nodded soberly.

"Fine. Then I'll pray last. And remember, kids, only pray for what you feel like Heavenly Father would want you to have."

Each of the children nodded, the family knelt in a small circle, and one by one they commenced to pour out their hearts to their God. And Sam was touched, maybe more so than he had ever been touched in his life. The prayers of his children were beautiful, thoughtful prayers, and he was amazed that these little ones could speak to the Lord as they did. Obviously that was because of Emily, who had knelt with them in prayer every morning and evening since before they had been old enough to speak.

Oh, he had done so occasionally himself, when he had been home. But his work had taken him away so often that, well, he knew that the credit for his children's spiritual strength should go to his wife, and that was squarely where he placed it.

When it was finally his turn, Sam thanked Heavenly Father for his family, and for their great faith. Then, as had his children before him, he pleaded that the lives of his wife and new baby might be spared. He was just concluding when the door burst open, and Jacob stood there with old Doc Steele in tow.

"Where is she?" the doctor asked as he stripped off his coat, hat, and scarf and tossed them on a chair.

Sam led him into the kitchen, the doctor plunged his hands into some warm water to get a little heat into them, and within another minute he was examining the almost unconscious Emily Chavez.

"Abby's right," he finally said softly as he turned to Sam. "There's trouble here, and I ain't smart enough to know exactly what it is. But one thing I do know, Sam. If I don't get that baby out of there pronto, it'll be dead."

"But how."

"I'll have to do a cesarean section on her, Sam. That's a surgical procedure where I make an incision and remove the baby through the abdomen."

"Will she . . . I mean Emily, will she be all right?"

For an instant or two the doctor hesitated. "Normally, yes," he finally answered. "But this ain't a normal situation, Sam. I've never seen this before, but I read of a case once that this brings to mind. Tell the truth, it looks to me like Emily's uterus has ruptured somewhere internally."

"That's bad?"

"Nothing worse, Sam. At best, she'll never have another baby. Just a shade the other side of best, she won't make it at all."

"But . . . why?"

"She'll have lost too much blood, Sam. I think she's losing it right now, and that's what's causing her spasms—blood puddling on the spinal column. So what's your decision? Do I try to save the baby and likely lose Emily quick, or do we just wait and let nature take its course and likely lose both of them?"

"I . . . I don't know, Doc. I . . ."

"Sam?" Emily called as if from a great distance. "The blessing? I need a blessing."

Blinking back tears, Sam looked at the doctor. "Will you anoint, Doc?"

The old man nodded. "My pleasure, Sam."

Taking the consecrated oil, Doctor Steele gently anointed Emily's head and stated that he did so by the authority of the Melchizedek Priesthood and in the name of Jesus Christ. Next Sam gently placed his hands on the head of his beloved companion, and with the doctor standing beside him, he pronounced a blessing upon her.

Never had Sam felt such a conflicting array of emotions— pain, grief, sorrow, anger, frustration, hopelessness—they were all churning around inside him. Yet despite them, never had he prayed so fervently that he might say only the words that God wanted him to say. He wanted his wife to live, he wanted his baby to live, and he knew that those were natural desires. Worse, he feared that one or both of them would die. But rather than pleading for their safety, Sam thought of the sweet prayers of his children, and he found himself simply speaking with his Divine Maker.

"Father," he said, after sealing the anointing, "things look mighty bleak for all of us today, and most especially for Em and the baby. But you know that anyway, don't you? Hadn't been for this storm, we might have gotten her to the hospital down in town. But you knew that already, too, even before you sent the storm. You're our Father, and you know all things, so you must've wanted Em to stay here at home. That's the only thing that makes sense, and believe me, Father, even then it doesn't make much.

"Anyhow, this is a hard place the Doc and Abby are in, so we bless both of them that their hands will be guided and that angels will help them to take care of Emily and the baby.

"We bless the baby that it . . . it . . . No sir, Heavenly Father, that baby isn't an 'it'! The Spirit says that this baby is a girl! We bless her then, this little girl, that she will have as long a life as she was promised before she ever left your presence, and we place her in your hands for the fulfillment of that promise.

"As for Em, well, Heavenly Father, you know how the

kids and I feel about this dear woman. To us it seems hardly possible that we can get along without her. And confound it, we don't want to, either! But, well, I've been raising my hand to the square for so many years in support of your earthly servants, and knowing I was doing right by it, that it'd be sort of foolish if I didn't do the same thing now. So Heavenly Father, my arm's to the square in support of whatever you think is best for my Emily—her and the rest of us, too. Doc says it'll take a miracle, and I know you have plenty of them on hand. But whether this is the time to use one up, well, the kids and I will leave that up to you.

"Meanwhile, dear Em, in the name of Jesus Christ we bless you that you won't suffer and that you will know how much all of us, Heavenly Father included, love you. Amen."

There was silence as Sam and Doctor Steele took their hands from Emily's head. Then she opened her eyes and looked up at her husband.

"Sam," she whispered, "kiss me . . . please."

Sam did so, tenderly and gently, telling his darling Em with every fiber of his being that he loved her. She responded weakly in kind, and it was only moments later that she closed her eyes in sleep. And so the grieving sheriff went out to sit with his children.

The next time Sam Chavez saw his bride, she had quietly passed away.

"I'm sorry, Sam," Doctor Steele said gently while Abby, her sobs muffled, busied herself with the still form of the baby. "I did all I knew how to do, and I still lost both of them. But that baby was a girl, all right. You sure had that one pegged."

"What happened?" Sam asked woodenly as he looked at the lifeless form of the woman he had come to love so dearly.

"The uterus, just like I feared. Somehow it had torn, and she and the little girl both bled to death. When I made the incision, well, blood spurted everywhere, and I just couldn't do a blamed thing to stop it."

"Did . . . did she suffer?"

"Emily? Not a bit, Sam, not after your blessing. She went to sleep right before you went out, and she never moved again. I saw when the blood stopped pumping, and when I checked, she was gone. She died real easy, Sam. I think the baby had died long before, too, as blue as she is. That means she didn't suffer anything either."

Doctor Steele moved off to help Abby, and Sam stood

alone with his grief, looking down at the strife-worn body that had so recently tabernacled his beloved companion. Fifteen years they had enjoyed each other's love and companionship, fifteen years that had been the happiest he had ever known. He and Emily would go on forever, he knew that, but for now he would have to settle for memories, and he just didn't know if he could do that.

On the back steps he blew his nose and tried to get himself under control, not so much because he wanted to be under control but because he needed to be with his children, and he needed to be strong for them as they worked their way through the loss of their mother.

Looking out at the barn, Sam realized that the wind had died and that the world had grown white and still. Well, at least the storm had subsided . . .

"Dear Father in Heaven," he prayed softly as he stood in the chilled afternoon air, "give me the strength to endure this trial. Help me to remember that she was yours before she was mine. I . . . I miss her . . . Oh, dear God how I miss her! Please take care of her for me.

"Emily? Em, sweetheart, I . . . I know you can hear me. Oh, how I wish it hadn't all ended so soon for us! You were the best thing that ever came down the pike for me—you and the kids. You take care of our little baby, you hear? I haven't had a chance to think of a name for her headstone—you were always the one with names. But I'll get it done, Em. Maybe I'll even name her after you. I just wish she could be here with us —to remind us all of you.

"I . . . I don't want you to go, sweetheart, but I reckon that Heavenly Father says it's time, and I don't suppose we can argue. Not effectively, anyhow. But Em, honey, don't go too far. I'll still be here, and only you know how badly I'll be needing your help!"

For a moment Sam Chavez screwed his eyes tightly closed while he rubbed at them with his fists. In his mind he could see his Emily, see her plainly, and she was pulling that little pout of hers that could get him out of the bluest funk in the world. But now it didn't work! Now he was alone without his beloved companion.

"Oh, Heavenly Father," he sobbed as he buried his face in his hands, "how can a man bear this sort of pain? It . . . it's like I'm all torn up in little chunks, all spread out, and every little chunk is hurting all by itself. I don't . . . I don't . . .

"Ahhh," he groaned softly as he turned to go back through the house to his children, "how does a man manage to do something he knows he can't ever on this green earth do? Father, you . . . you've got to help me know what to say to the little ones."

"Sarah, Mary, Jake, Adam, and Nick," he said sadly a few moments later as he gathered his five weeping children into his arms, "Heavenly Father has asked your mommy and your baby sister to come home to him. That means he needs them bad, and so, as much as it hurts, each of us has to be willing to let them go . . ."

"Sam? Sam?"

Sam and his children all turned toward the anxious voice of old Doctor Steele. And all were surprised to see him coming through the doorway from the kitchen, a tiny bundle in his hands, and a red-eyed but beaming Abigale Wagner following behind.

"Sam, would you take a look at this? Abby just wouldn't quit on this little darling and now just look at her. A minute ago she just up and started breathing, and I believe she's going to make it!"

Instantly Sarah was on her feet, her hands held out. "I'll take her, Doc," she said, sounding so much like her mother that Sam almost jumped. "Mary, get some diapers, and Jake, you get that stove stoked up before this poor little tyke catches her death of cold. Adam, you help your brother. Now I—"

Suddenly nine-year-old Sarah noticed her father. "I . . . I'm sorry, Daddy," she apologized, appearing terribly embarrassed. "I shouldn't have given orders like that."

But Sam was on his feet, holding his eldest and youngest daughters close to him. "Sarah," he replied gently, "you might add a *please* in there, but otherwise you did just what your mother would have done. Little Emily here is going to need lots of love and care, and if we all work hard as we can, I think she'll turn out just like Mother wants her to. And believe you me, she wanted this little one here with us!

"Now hop to it, boys. While you're stoking the stove, I'll get some fresh warm milk out of old Hepsibah, and we'll see if little Em is ready to eat."

While Sarah sat in the rocker and the other children scurried on their errands, Sam Chavez walked back into the kitchen, where he gently took the hand of his beloved wife.

"Thanks, Em," he said softly as he caressed her skin, new tears blurring his eyes as he did so. "And thank Heavenly Father for me, too. It'll be tough as nails, but with little Em here to remind all of us that you . . . that you're still about and loving us, well, you have my word on it, Emily Chavez, we're going to make it!

"And say, Em. Did you notice how cute that little tyke turned out to be? Some day some poor fella is going to be worse struck than I was when first I laid eyes on you."

Authors' Note

Though the storm we have been following is long gone, as are the people caught up in it, similar storms continue to buffet us mortals continually. While these may be weather related, most likely they will not. Weather related or not, justified or not, these continuing storms of life will present us with problems, difficulties, sorrow, and pain. Under such conditions, as did the people in the foregoing stories, we will best meet the challenges presented us if we will turn to the Lord. Then will our afflictions have, as Alma said, "truly humbled" us.

Better still, if we will wholeheartedly turn to the Lord even when no storms are present, the storms that come later will be less severe and we will be better prepared to meet them. As Alma asked of the poverty-stricken Zoramites, "Do ye not suppose that they are more blessed who truly humble themselves?"

With Alma, we conclude, "Yea, he that truly humbleth himself, and repenteth of his sins, and endureth to the end, the same shall be blessed—yea, much more blessed than they who are compelled to be humble." (Alma 32:6, 13–15.)

Sources Consulted

Anderson, Bette Roda. *Weather in the West.* Palo Alto, Calif.: American West Publishing Company, 1975.

Eubank, Mark E., and Clayton R. Brough. *Mark Eubank's Utah Weather.* Salt Lake City: Weatherbank, Inc., 1979.

Eubank, Mark E. *Snowbank's Little Weather Book.* Salt Lake City: Weatherbank, Inc., 1986.

Mason, Elda Copley. *Lasqueti Island, History and Memory.* Victoria, British Columbia, Canada: AdMan Printing, Ltd., 1976.

Rubin, Louis D., Sr., and Jim Duncan. *The Weather Wizard's Cloud Book.* Chapel Hill, North Carolina: Algonquin Books, 1984.

Sinclair, Bertrand W. *Poor Man's Rock.* Toronto, Ontario, Canada: The Ryerson Press, 1920.

Whipple, A.B.C. *Storm, Planet Earth.* Alexandria, Virginia: Time-Life Books, 1982.